D0499802

Astrology &
Sexual Analysis

Morris C. Goodman

Melvin Powers
Wilshire Book Company

12015 Sherman Road, No. Hollywood, CA 91605

contents

(illustrations appear after page 90)

"This is the Age of Aquarius."
Here you have the title of a song from *Hair,* a play with music which has been a long-running, record-breaking hit. In the production, the entire cast makes an appearance in the nude. In New York and the other world capitals where this play is on the boards, there have been no outcries from the professional reformers nor any protests by the ministry nor any arrests of the producers or performers.

Why, when Mae West served a thirty day sentence for using one expression found to be obscene in her play, *Sex,* only a generation ago? At about the same time, the licenses of all burlesque theatres were revoked in New York City.

Why is *Hair* running with no interference? The answer is self-contained in the title of the hit song; this *is* the Age of Aquarius.

With the ending of World War II, the Aquarian Age began; it is the new cycle of the brotherhood of man and of enlightenment. What characteristics has it manifested thus far? Leading off with the A's, astrology has become a world-wide craze, fad, hobby, profession, pursuit. Call it what you will, it is dominating social life and profoundly affecting industry. It has become the quasi-religion of the under-thirty generation, and is the universal topic of conversation.

Formerly hounded underground by fear—not law—astrologers are doing a thriving business; radio, television, and the press are gasping for time to fill the public's demands for more and more information about the influence of the planets.

Is astrology valid? The writer has complete belief in it. The reader may find the pro's and con's in dozens of dissertations on the shelves of his nearest library. This is not the subject of this book.

This book deals with sexuality. It is a revelation of astrology's encyclopedic analysis of sex and personality, about love in all its natural forms and aberrations. Its purpose is to enable you to understand yourself and others, and to understand the greatest driving force in life itself: sexuality.

"To know all is to understand all."

M.C.G.

New York City

THE ROLE OF SEX IN THE AGE OF AQUARIUS

The oldest recorded astrology is that of the Chinese. The historians' educated guess is that astrology may be 40,000 years old, having Tibet as its birthplace. In Chinese mythology, interwoven with astrology, is the story of creation. According to it, God created the earth, then man. Man went to God and told Him he was lonely, that he could not live alone. So God created woman, to give man a companion.

Soon the man and woman began to quarrel. The man went to God again. This time, he said, "I cannot live with woman. Take her away." God took her away. Then man became very depressed. He went to God and beseeched Him to return woman to him.

God said to man, "You see, you cannot live with woman, and you cannot live without her. This will be your destiny until the end of time."

This is a simple tale. It took place in an uncomplicated world which became complex, antagonistic, and contradictory as soon as there were two sexes in it.

11

The male principle is symbolized by the Sun in astrology, the female by the Moon. This may be the first occult knowledge ever acquired by humans. It is perfectly rational, makes excellent sense, and it substantiates the tenets of astrology. Without solar radiation there would be absolutely no life on the planet earth. The Moon takes a month in the celestial calendar to transit the twelve Signs of the zodiac; it is the time-keeper of the menstrual period or monthly.

Leaping forward in time some unnumbered centuries, we find further complications in the love-sex situation. In *The Symposium* of Plato, the dichotomy of love is expounded. This reveals three (or an addition of two) kinds of love: the love of man for woman; the love of woman for woman; the love of man for man. It ends "and the greatest of these is the love of man for man." This was in conformity to the mores and customs of the times. It is an expression of the Sun-plus-Sun creative astrological principle. The product, the creation, was the noble friendship in battle and the philosophy which led to the foundation and maintenance of the first city-state.

The man-woman love was the Sun-Moon influence or fertility—conception principle required for reproduction, and for survival of the race. This was the essential of the marriage rite in the community. The lesbian relationship was the Moon-plus-Moon influence, barren without the solar influence, "dead"—as the Moon is dead.

Even this Greek civilized pattern or complex seems simple nowadays. Let no one think that the complexities of today's sexual permissiveness were either unknown or not practiced in other times. One would be deluded to think there was no masturbation, narcissism, sadism, masochism, fetishism, cunilingus, pederasty, Oedipus complexes, Electra complexes, sibling love, incest, actual master-slave relationships, self-flagellation, or sexual abstinence. There were simply no names for them or other names. It took Sigmund Freud and his followers to create a new vocabulary to christen practices known thousands of years before his time. Some were condemned or permitted depending on the astrological Age of Man. All are with us now.

What is sex in the Age of Aquarius? It is the same act of copulation reaching orgasm within a few minutes that it was thousands of years ago. It is, in its climax of orgasm, an experience affecting sixty nerve centers in the human body. It is the most talked about experience, the most sought after experience. It is the strongest driving force of humanity. Anatole France derided the importance humans place on the sexual act because of its repetitious monotony and brevity compared to the hours' long hermaphroditic, sadomasochistic sexual thrills of the snail!

Why, then, all the talk, all the discussion, all the words about sex in newspapers and magazines, in movies, plays, books, bedrooms, and courts of law? It is not all about the same old thing. It's about what's new about it — understanding sex, finding a way to sexual happiness and to understanding attitudes to sex in the Astro-Space Age.

All of these matters concern people. And astrology is concerned with people, their happiness potential, and their improvement through the understanding of themselves which astrology gives them.

We might mention animals, too, as they concern people in several ways. First, it should be made clear that references elsewhere to man's animal nature or the animal side of his nature are very libelous to animals. Sex in animals is far more orderly than it is in humans; certainly, it is up to and probably surpasses man's moral standards. Most animals are monogamous, model parents with model families. Sex plays a role as a preliminary to reproduction and the preservation of the species, but that role is, of course, in the nature of sensation. In the classification of the species of the animal kingdom each has its astrological ruling planet.

Animals are the friends, enemies, servants, and food of man. As pets they play a great role in human emotions. In cases of (criminal) bestiality, many aspects in the individual's chart must be analyzed to give a clear understanding of this condition which may be more prevalent than is commonly known.

This is, however, but one of the strange practices of modern times. The Age of Aquarius is filled with complexes or "hangups" as the rising generation calls them.

Uniquely, the terms 'sacred' and 'profane' love are still used; the former is ruled by Venus, the latter by Pluto. The problems of homosexual tendencies and homosexual panic run rampant through these times of permissiveness, and they are ruled by various aspects of Mars, Neptune, and the Moon. Personal codes individually created in opposition to conventional codes and partially attributable to Dr. Alfred Adler and his school of "individual psychology" are ruled by the Sun and Mars.

Changing moral standards throughout the world are responsible for changing sexual habits. This is particularly true in the United States where the changes have been more sudden than in nations labeled corrupt, such as Germany where permissivenes and perversion were rampant following World War I. These changes are under the rulership of Uranus (upgrading), Pluto (downgrading), and Saturn (changes due to time).

The "generation gap" is under the rulership of Saturn, and this slowly moving planet, characterized as the "celestial school-master", has produced some unique ideas on sex, especially pre-marital relations. Typical of Saturn's influence, people asked in a Gallup poll in the over-thirty age group considered such sex relations wrong in the majority of cases. Those between twenty and thirty were divided about evenly. College students approved pre-marital sex two to one. Adult whites were overwhelmingly against such relations while adult Negroes were divided about evenly. More women were against than in favor, this group being also under the influence of the Moon as well as Saturn, while males are under the influence of the Sun and Mars as well as Saturn to a preponderant degree. The latter qualifying statement is included, as every individual has every planet in his or her individual horoscope.

The above opinions were collected in a Gallup poll taken in 1969. The institute of Sex Research where Dr. Albert Kinsey compiled his provocative Report issued the opinion that the "now" generation has changed more in its attitude towards sex than in its behavior pattern.

Many women play the role of the mistress of a man, in some cases both parties thinking that there is some form of status in their position. Here one has an example of the influence of Venus, Saturn, and Mars. In upper-class society where such a relationship may take on an air of being chic or fashionable, an aspect of the power of Mercury would also be in evidence.

The sexual instinct is a very powerful force under the rulership of Venus for both sexes, Mars for the male, and the Moon for the female. Yet under Plutonian radiation it is being attacked and evinced in such seeming but effective byways as the appearance of the anti-hero, the anti-war pacifist, the drug addict, and the alcoholic—all types who are losing expression of the sex force.

The feminization of the male, especially in America, has become one of the most serious and widespread characteristics of sex in the Aquarian Age. It would appear that if ever there was a "battle of the sexes", the female sex has won! The ascendancy is witnessed or observable in the feminized male, the crucial love relationships of people in life and their reflections in films, drama, and books, the painful sense of failure in the people attending psychiatric or therapeutic sessions, the docility of the male spouse, and the confessed absence of sexual passion in the night people, the hippies, the hipsters, and the yippies. Sexual envy plays a great part in this picture: the women seem to be dominating the home, the business world, the world of finance, and are rising higher and higher in the world of politics; the males seem to be regressive, docile, despairing, and their sex is increasingly turning to homosexuality and trans-sexual operations. One might say a mighty switch is taking place.

One cannot but agree with the greatest of modern sexologists, Dr. Robert S. De Ropp, that "man is almost insanely sexual." But one might add that this is more of a modern manifestation than an old one, or one of older times.

The next section of this book reveals sexual tendencies by Signs. It is important to remember that every planet is in every Sign. Hence a Sign reading is based only on the position of the Sun at birth. There is an interpretation for each sex born under each Sign. These analyses are followed by a Sexual Compatibility Guide describing the sex potential of the Signs to each other.

Aries: March 21 to April 19

THE ARIES MALE

March 21st to April 19th

The symbol of Aries is the Ram. The origin of this zodiacal beast is the season of fertility, the spring. The constellation's pattern seemed to form the outline of a ram in the days when shepherds in the fields looked up to the darkening skies. It is an apposite symbol, for the ram with the small "r" is a synonym for a device which batters, crushes, drives or forces something, and this is characteristic of the Aries male. He is a real man. Even the homosexual Aries male has masculine physical characteristics, rarely any secondary feminine traits.

Men born under Aries do not deceive the astrologer. Their exteriors may be very tough, and most likely they are, and they are hard-boiled in their business dealings, but they long for true, romantic love. They melt at love given to them selflessly and generously. They mourn bitterly when the affair is over.

The Aries male's sexual appetite is enormous. His qualifications for being the love machine are right there, and he is just about ever ready. In youth, sex bewilders him, and he seeks a happy attachment with someone who understands his blind groping and is patient enough to teach him, console him for the accidents and heartbreaks of adolescence, and loves him until he is ready to enter the grown-up phase of sex.

Satyriasis can become his personal complex because he is a born hunter, but one with the instincts of a ferret. He can almost smell out his prey, and prey it is likely to become—whether a member of the opposite sex or his own. Having chosen the object of his sexual desires, he pursues it relentlessly. Nor is he satisfied with a single sexual act or orgasm. The first may indeed act only as a stimulant, arousing his passion to an uncontrollable degree. Should he be repulsed after the initial act, it would drive him to seek still another partner, and he would not give up until he succeeded in finding one.

The male of the Sign Aries tends to be well built to go with his own aggressive nature. Unless, however, he takes particular pains with his grooming, his clothing, and especially his skin, he will not make a successful impression. For conquest, therefore, it is wise for him to take special care of every detail of his appearance. He should shave daily, and he may have to repeat this for special neatness in the evening; his linen and suits should be fresh and pressed at all times. This will prevent his seeming overbearing because of his powerful sexual drive or his natural physique. Diet and exercise are prescribed to prevent early fleshiness and flabbiness. Health and its glow will also subtract attention from the eyes which are, or seem, small or beady in the Aries male.

They can carry bodily development to foolish extremes, and the beach boys, body builders, and exhibitionists at the beach are likely to be their Sign siblings.

The planetary influences generally give them over-average height, and they develop a ruddy complexion topped by thick eyebrows colored to match some shade of black hair which usually thins in the middle years of life.

They do not separate their vocation from their sexual life, seeking partners (as they do everywhere) in the office, at conventions, and on business trips or at combined social-business functions. Without self-control, they can gamble (and lose), due to allowing the negative side of Aries dominate. They can overindulge in alcohol, and let their moral censor slip to the point of engaging in unethical or dishonest business deals.

The views of the Aries males change as they mature, and the liberalism of youth changes to conservatism in later life. They may sigh over the lost idealism of youth, but they enjoy the material benefits of their conversion. The benefits make it possible to induce lovelier partners to go to bed with them. They don't like to consider this paying for "it", but in their secret hearts they know that is what they are doing. They should not hide from themselves nor think that the cultivation of highbrow interests (natural to them) will subtract from the powerful drive of their sexual desires.

Traditional astrology attributes heroism to them in military life, but modern astrology declares that their eyes wander to the form and beauty and the men or women with whom they share such a life. Their hypnotic sexual power, aggression, and will to succeed can subdue their superior officers or even enslave them for the time being.

The Aries male can make his mate very happy because his inclination is to be generous and thoughtful. He can also torment his mate by being jealous, demanding, questioning and allowing no time for independent action no

21

matter how innocent. His conduct can be infantile or childish when he feels neglected. This is a hangover from excessive mother love, (something he carries all through life), and he unconsciously seeks his mother in his mate. To sire a large brood can be his hope, dream or ambition, plus which the "pill" is anathema to him.

Because the Aries male is very sensitive beneath his warlike exterior, Mars being his planetary Ruler, he is subject to psychosomatic disorders. Domestic strife can bring on painful symptoms, e.g., headache, asthma, constriction of the chest. These are caused by emotional stress and tension, sexual frustration, and can lead to heart weakness, especially if he is a heavy drinker or smoker. Hypnosis works very effectively to stop the latter practices but is ineffectual in sublimating sexual cravings.

"Stormy Weather" could be the theme song of the Aries male's sexual and emotional life. When he is at the zenith of happiness in a love affair, he questions his good luck and jumps from ecstasy to despair and back again. He finds it impossible to accept happiness completely, and this is the clue to his romantic misery. He must learn to enjoy it while it lasts; it may well be the hardest lesson in his life, but it would prove of infinite value. He must also learn that his passions control him, not he them, for desire can lead him to costly experiences, expensive to purse, health and reputation.

The Arian has the ability to win those in the most cultured sectors of society and is just as happy rutting with an unlettered woman. Yet he tells himself he wants happiness, a kind which comes from mutual love! This will come to him only as a reward for learning the meaning of and the acquisition of total, personal unselfishness. Difficult, but worth it.

THE ARIES FEMALE

March 21st to April 19th

The Aries female loves sex, and once she has discovered it—at whatever age, and usually an early one—she can become crazy about it. She develops a craving for knowledge of the erotic. Her interests will be concentrated on a study of male and female anatomy, and she is aroused to extremes by the actual appearance and size of her partner's sexual organs. This woman reads books on sex, erotica, and pornography with a keen eye. She becomes a collector of stimuli, from ticklers to photographs to the instruments used by sadists and masochists.

In the emotions involved in sex, the Aries female chooses true love and wishes above all things to be its object. Her lover must be demonstrative above all things if he (or she) does not want a complaining, nagging, frustrated woman on hand. She is ever ready, publicly or privately, to be told she is loved, to be petted, pinched, stroked, felt, patted, kissed, and excited.

The Aries female deludes herself thoroughly about the one she loves—until disillusion sets in. She endows her lover with traits, characteristics and qualities her love never possessed. This astrological type sees wonders in the commonest partner in her sex life, she interprets the simplest gesture of politeness as one of regal condescension or the sharing of some royal and secret compact of amorous intrigue. When her eyes are opened, the abyss and the fall thereinto are all the more disastrous.

Restlessness and impatience are traits of the Aries woman, and their roots are in her sexual desires, which seem insatiable. They are evinced in social and business conduct, but they stem from her external heat. The intellectual Aries female sublimates this infinite energy into creative channels. Nevertheless, when the zenith of desire overtakes the sublimation, she will devour her mate or seek experiences by picking one up in the nearest bar, park, or on the corner.

Often a cause of unhappiness to the Aries female is the fact that men do not understand her or take her seriously. The first impression she makes may be one of stupidity—not necessarily a true or accurate impression at all! Her appearance may exaggerate this as light coloring may make her one of those blondes whom "gentlemen prefer"— but marry brunettes (with a bow to Anita Loos). The blonde who was immortalized by that fine writer presented a naive stupidity to her prey and profound cupidity to her mirror. However, she seeks to please, enjoys sex, and gives as good as she gets.

The Aries woman has the aggressive quality just as much as the Aries man. She can forge ahead in social life, society (which is quite different), the theater and movies, the cosmetics industry, and the world where beauty itself is an industry, fashion, contests, and perhaps political intrigue. This girl begins to gather prizes at an early age, and they may be admirers, lovers, helpmeets, husbands, partners, and in some cases, victims. She dotes on overcoming all males and can act so cleverly that the number of males who make up her list of successes or conquests is very large. If she decides to make a conquest, nothing will remain standing in her way, and her batting average will be .1000!

The equipment possessed by the Aries female makes her an early starter, for her feminine attributes develop when young, and she presents a picture of voluptuous sexuality perhaps even before she understands either her own attractions or the mysteries of sex. She looks appetizing by the time she celebrates that old-fashioned birthday, sweet sixteen, with breasts upstanding, a waist a man can slip his arm around, sensuous hips, and a walk like Marilyn Monroe's. At this age she begins to collect scalps—and proudly, too. The upper body resembles an inverted pyramid, slightly like that of the Aries athlete. As she grows older, she may tend towards acquiring fat, but she is the kind to fight it with gadgets, diet, exercise, and self-control.

With Mars, that red, hot, and fiery planet as the Ruler of Aries, the woman born under this Sign will frequently find herself in complicated situations. The secret and adventurous places, the haunts of the underground, the exotic locales, and dangerous territory all lure her, nor does she resist the temptations that they offer. What she finds, she wants; what she wants, she also wants to rule. While relationships thus formed may be casual, temporary, or one-night stands, the physical aspects that accompany this kind of anonymous affair can release hidden repressions and explode into a sexuality with all its rare perversities indulged in with either a male or female partner.

Besides the physical endowments of the Aries

woman, her charm is enhanced by the variety of interests, the outward-going facets of her personality, and her ability to acquire numerous skills. She is attracted to the novel, to activities that are really innovations, and this makes her seek out new or young talent as well as to be very attractive to it. There is nothing square about her attitudes except her acquisitive trait, and she fairly sneers at people who retain established ways of thinking, standards now ignored, and outmoded moral and political codes. In this freedom she somehow clings to superstition, an inconsistency that is most amusing—yet she clings to it. The lady might disclaim such a foolish characteristic while saying, "I'm not superstitious knock wood!"

A troublesome part of the Aries woman's social and sexual life is a deep, perhaps consciously hidden, sensitivity. This leads to misunderstandings which are painful to her and the other person concerned. A fault, a failure to remember some anniversary, a seeming slight—perhaps even unknown to the "guilty" party—can produce a display of temper that is shocking and uncalled for. Or it will produce a pout that can be long, emotionally expensive, and even end in active enmity. The Aries lady will not welcome an invitation to talk things over. She will either suddenly dismiss the whole disagreement or send some elaborate and costly gift as a form of apology.

This Aries female has a terrific sense of humor and appreciation of wit, but not a well-developed sense of fun. She seems almost too big for foolish fun and games, yet can laugh louder than anyone else at the party. A great story-teller, she can be the most sarcastic sneerer at people who fail to get the point of the joke she has told.

In the biography of this lady, there is usually one

life-long admirer somewhere in the background. Through memory, nostalgia, sentiment, maybe true love, there is one man or one love in the background who is forever enamored with her and eternally loyal. She has the good sense as well as the sensitivity to appreciate this, and pays some kind of respect to the gift and its giver. Her motive may not be the highest, for in her secret heart she may selfishly be whispering, "Who knows? Some day I may need him."

Marriage may seem remote from the traits ascribed to the daughter of Aries, but it is as though this is a separate department, one which she can control, steer to success, and keep safely separate from all other departments of life. She can inspire as well as drive her mate to success. She usually bears many children, so financial success is really imperative. Her instincts as a mother are most admirable, and she can love husband and offspring while never being deceived about their faults or their weaknesses. Attractive to the end of a usually long life, the Aries woman will be a man-killer right up to her last breath.

Taurus: April 20 to May 20

♉

THE TAURUS MALE

April 20th to May 20th

A great deal of astrology can be absorbed from the symbolism of the planets and the Signs. The symbol for the Sign of Taurus is the Bull, one of the beasts of the natural zodiac (from the Greek, zoion, animal). It is, indeed, a curiosity, for the symbol is far more applicable to the male of the Sign than to the female. It is indicative of a very powerful sexual ability, a great physique, a diversified mating—all those traits brought to mind by the expression in common usage, "built like a bull."

While the social conduct of the Taurus male can be quite like that of the animal which symbolizes him, it can also be very sophisticated. This is because he is a quick learner, a man with tremendous native intelligence, and able to absorb the culture and manners of any environment with ease. The veneer may be magnificent, but the below surface crashing urges and violence are there. It may take shock, anger, or overpowering desire to reveal what many coats of lacquer conceal—but there they are.

One of the grand games of astrology people play is

"guessing your Sign." Perhaps the Taurus male is the easiest to guess, for he is rarely able to conceal his true self from one with normal intuitive perception. He may be of humble origins, a poor family, a city boy or a country boy. His aim, whatever his natal surroundings, is success. He may have magnetic qualities to bring him sexual success with beautiful partners. If he hasn't, he will dream of such great accomplishments that he will gain his ideal through power or wealth.

It is the sexual urge that drives him to seek material success, for he knows that with it he can control the destinies of men, women, and children. Not uniquely, he may choose some avenue of great artistic creativity as a way of gaining wealth because the ruling planet of his Sign is Venus. This planetary rulership does not necessarily make him a creative genius; he may be one. Should he not be, he will align himself with people who are, manage them, direct them, promote them, use them, abuse them, and in the end make them produce while he pockets the largest percentage of their earnings. This may make him a largely unsavory character, but it has some good in it. It simultaneously—if painfully—spurs on his associates or victims to greater and greater creative, productive, and profitable efforts.

When one has identified a Taurus male, one will begin to notice certain very enduring traits revealed in unconscious movements and gestures. He seeks to provoke others to talk rather than do the talking, when he has some specific aim or gain in view. His thinking here is that the other party will talk himself or herself into a binding situation that will cost the Taurean less than if he made an offer. The goods being bargained over may be material, artistic, or services—commercial or sexual. Rarely will he say, "I offer you . . . ."

He can wait until the other party says, "I want . . . ." Or he may ask, "How much?"

One should not gather the impression that this man is not talkative or articulate. That is his bargaining mask. During this dialogue, he will keep his antagonist from closeness, from approaching him. Between them, the Taurean will set up barriers. He will hold out his cigarette, point with his pen or pencil, remove his eye-glasses and point the ear-pieces at the other person. Unconsciously fighting a duel in which only he is armed, he chooses all these articles—all phallic symbols—because with any one of them he is going to triumph over the other party.

When necessary, and other ploys have failed, he can talk, talk, and talk. He will try to win the contest by sheer overbearing repetition to get the dotted line signed or the prey into his bed. During this demonstration he plays scales of monologues, up, down, persuasive, acting all parts in some story, revealing his culture in a wealth of classical allusions, shocking with the sudden use of some obscene expression. That is the Bull in him, the Bull who is kicking up the turf, getting ready for the charge. The date or time set, now relaxed, he becomes the great story-teller, he thinks. His anecdotal repertory goes on and on. His boring recital is interrupted by sudden flashes of conversational brilliance. He will create and relate interminable fantasies giving each of them his certified testimonial of truth. All going back to his symbolic beast.

The Taurus male has a disarming appearance, for it conceals his extreme emotional-sexual nature. Rarely less than average height, he maintains through nature or self-control a good figure. The face is neither broad nor narrow, with the lips compressed and the hair thinned out as time takes its toll. With unique vigor that seems eternal, the eyes alone may show signs of age, with pouches, or wrinkles, or small skin blemishes.

This man is a hard worker, legal or religious holidays making no difference to his non-hour daily or week-end schedule. The excessive energy of the sex drive is redirected into superior business ability or social ambitions, but not so inclusively as to omit pleasures, especially sexual enjoyment. The driving and primary force is always to sex. Even his business trips and vacations are not without the search and the hope for a sexual conquest.

The Taurus man wants gratification first, therefore marriage may have little significance for him other than as a status symbol. The Taurean of lowly origin will happily marry above his station in early life, but not necessarily make his wife's life a happy one. Should she be unable to satisfy his insistent demands, he will seek other partners and be most careless of his mate's discovery of his other affairs. Nor will her jealousy or scenes upset him, for he has a built-in insulation to such signs of temperament.

Children are in about the same relationship to the Taurus married man. He has a curiosity and intellectual interest in his offspring, but no profound emotional relationship with them. He will be helpful, proud of their accomplishments, interested in their liberation, and instructive as long as they will learn to follow in his footsteps. He could easily make a play for another woman with his daughter by his side, even pushing her off on some man to have a bit of fun. Unless his son followed in his footsteps, he would consider such a child a rather stupid chap. All this leaves the Taurus male's legal mate in the position of having to accept him as he is with the benefits which accrue to her or of having to leave him and lose her social position.

With all his maleness and concentration on sexual pleasure, the Taurus male rarely deviates by joining in sex with another male or in other than the straight sex act with a female. He may try either of these variations but hardly like either one or become addicted to such practices. Uniquely for such a domineering male, he is not critical or upset by the unfaithfulness of his mistress or mistresses, but can become pathetically jealous of one woman whom he comes to regard as his private property. This even though she is married to some other man. She becomes a symbol of his achievement if she is especially pleasing or accomplished in sex or represents the conquest of some seemingly unattainable "lady" with a position in "high society."

The rulership of Venus over Taurus gives rise to some engrossing frustrations. The Venus-ruled Taurean may earnestly desire fame as a fiction or play writer. More likely this would develop as an avocation. His aim: fame. For fame brings the admiration of women. As a playwright, it would make beautiful stars available to him. Rather untalented actors and athletes might fight their way to the top with the same aim driving them on.

The early life of the Taurus male may not be very happy. He seems to have some conflict between the attention necessary to the growth of his mind and that of his body. The tremendous impact on the sexual drive in the body is a force most difficult to control. It may take precedence over all other drives; it may cause the young "Bull" to seek sexual gratification through young girls or female relatives, even though acts of aggression are required.

The object of the youthful Taurus male's search may

be females of retarded mental development. Being conscious of his own lack of knowledge, technique, and sophistication, he wisely or instinctively pursues the prey he realizes is easiest to catch!

The Taurus male looks forward to a long life and one filled with sexual satisfaction. His sex vision is generally 20/20, and he rarely veers to any form of aberration. His potency becomes a mental problem in later life, which in turn can bring about psychic impotence. However, he responds beautifully to injections of hormones. This gives him both psychic confidence and the physical ability to spend the golden years of his life as he would have wished to all his life.

April 20th to May 20th

In contrast with the traits of the male member of the Taurus family, the female, although her Sign's zodiacal beast is also the Bull, is typically feminine. She has the appearance of gentle and genteel femininity, built small, with large eyes in a rather compact face, wearing a look of critical seriousness. She is studious about life and sex, perusing its vagaries in an academic and scholarly manner.

The woman born under Taurus accepts motherhood with a kind of careless grace. She can take it or leave it and be equally happy either way, but would show a preference for daughters.

While she strives for personal beauty, it is for the sake of beauty itself rather than to make her sexually attractive to men. The rulership of Venus over the Sign Taurus sways the female more in the direction of beauty than of love. In choosing vocations the Taurus lady tends to those which enhance the beauty of the body. She would more likely become a make-up expert, theatrical dresser, or designer than a star. Coordinated fields are career guidance, teaching, hotel management, hostess work (in restaurants, clubs, on ships and planes). She can earn a good living through the use of her natural, innate charm. In so doing, she is very helpful to others, particularly members of her own sex.

This all seems very sublimated and high-minded, controlled, and far from the overpowering force of sex. While it is true, it does not exclude the force of sex. Rather the two parts of the personality co-exist. For the Taurus female has a tremendous sex drive and is a potential nymphomaniac—which part of her nature she conceals beneath her demure exterior and helpful actions.

In circumstances or situations away from her conventional environment, the Taurus woman reveals her true nature—her love for sexual pleasure. The Taurus male has neither curiosity nor interest in sexual abberations and deviations; not so the Taurus female. She has both an avid curiosity and a profound interest in all the forms and variations sex offers for thrills. The notorious "leather girl" of New Jersey represents the extreme of this type who enjoy sadistic pleasures, beating men, satisfying their lusts in torturing the male and forcing him into satisfying her lusts with all kinds of weird and far-out acts of perversion. At the other end of the Taurus scale is the sadistic female who searches far and wide for a partner who will force her into sexual slavery, overpowering her into the lowest forms of obnoxious and disgusting acts—which she thoroughly enjoys. Both of these extremes of Taurus personalities are capable of marrying, gradually impressing upon their spouses the roles which will gain them the sexual gratification which they crave. Both are capable of evolving a contemptuous attitude towards their mates should the latter fail to respond or lose his potency or interest. Both are capable of seeking and finding other sexual partners for their perverse pleasures.

There is a lot of self-love in the Taurus female. As the woman emerges from the girl, her interest in herself increases. Gradually she comes to love her body and its image in the mirror. She is willing to exercise, diet, ride horseback, take dancing lessons, spend a lot on cosmetics and even submit to surgery in straining for greater and greater embellishment. Only a unique pattern of the planets in her chart would ever make the Taurus female a lover of her own sex.

The woman of Taurus likes comfort, luxury, and elegance in her surroundings. She will intuitively furnish her boudoir in a manner to go with her sexual tastes. In her closets can be found anything from perfumes to whips, in her medicine cabinet, all the known cosmetic aids.

To friends and family, the Taurus woman displays her charm, concealing her potent sex drive. She appears, and really is, amiable with a deep ability to attract people without being ostentatious or talkative or demonstrative. She has such a subtle quality of power that people volunteer to do her will or even to anticipate her wishes and fulfill them.

There is a great deal of temperament, both nervous and artistic, in the Taurus woman's personality. The Venus influence in her chart creates a drive towards artistic achievement and the potential gains of fame and fortune. She might strive to become a great singer or actress but succeed only in becoming a great manager of singers, or a great dress or costume designer, or wardrobe mistress. The latter success, however, would hardly satisfy her, although few people would ever learn of her secret frustration. Having earthy qualities, she garners such success and nurtures it while striving in privacy for her real aim in life. This entire extension of personality can be applied to her sex life, marriage, or love life. To the world, all these (or any one) would be presented as a picture of exemplary happiness. In private she might be consorting with a man from the toughest background striving for perfection in sexual activity to achieve the greatest possible physical excitement out of her body.

The Taurus-born woman is well aware of her attractive traits, and she does all she can to make men aware of them, too. She puts on a great show although the performance might be somewhat unpredictable. Woman friends who entertain her are quite likely to say, while awaiting her arrival, "I wonder what she'll wear tonight." And she can arrive and make a surprise spectacular appearance by showing up looking like the most feminine, dreamy, whipped-cream-edible sweet thing in the world—or like a severely tailored, sophisticated, cold, brilliant but calculating courtesan. In either garb, she's going to be a knockout, always will provide a surprise or a little shock, and never be less than stimulating. Stimulating women to a bit of envy, men to erect attention.

While the lady has great powers of analysis, and can understand herself and other people, she might just make one error in judgment. She may fail to realize that her Shirley Temple pose will bring her men who provide greater sexual gratification than her Marlene Dietrich pose.

Endurance, while more difficult for the male to maintain, is a great trait of the Taurus female. She is the ardor of Nabakov's Ada, able to receive the male for long bouts of sexual intercourse, and retaining a high emotional temperature throughout. This woman realizes that male members of most Sign Groups do not have the stamina, potency, or training to keep up the act as long as she can nor as long as she desires. For this reason, she is able to study the art of love, to learn all about how to make a man take longer, come back to erection after orgasm, or to slow his action to make the contact last longer. What she really considers an ideal lover is an East Indian who has been instructed in youth in the fabled method of maintaining an erection for eight hours. This would be the Taurus woman's dream man! How she even enjoys reading about some movie star, this prize of sex, this paramour steeped in the art of love. How she enjoys the scandalous adventures he experienced, and envies the women he drove to madness with his tantalizing proclivities. And so she studies books on the techniques of sex and subtly trains her partners in ways to bring her to the zenith of ecstasy and the heights of repeated screaming orgasm.

This Sign rules the throat and the area surrounding it, and it is for this reason that Sign members are reputedly the greatest in number to indulge in practices which bring about pleasure and climax through oral contact. Experienced practitioners, (both the active and passive partner) realize the oral act can be prolonged and repeated with far greater frequency and greater excitation than the normal act. It creates a kind of sexual frenzy reaching dizzying heights, and practiced mutually in the "notorious" *soixante-neuf* (69) position brings on a form of slavery from which the slaves wish never to be freed.

With all her desires, and the will to attain them, the Taurus woman can lead a lonely life. She is essentially idealistic, really seeking her one and only true mate. But while she is seeking, she experiments, tries living with a man, has cycles of depression or turns to other outlets for her energies. In the end, sublimation of sex energy will not be her cure, and back she'll go to the bed—and not alone.

Gemini: May 21 to June 20

♊

THE GEMINI MALE

The sexual analysis of the men born under the Sign of Gemini is complicated but not confusing. It is so because Gemini is a Double Sign. In traditional astrology this has been taken to mean a dual personality, or two entities born under the influence of a single planet. The world has had folk tales and myths, and even children's rhymes, about this subject. One can read of Castor and Pollux, Romulus and Remus, Cain and Abel, even Adam and Eve, as being associated with the twins (sic) in the astrological symbol for Gemini, with which Sign these figures have been associated by astrologers. And one can recall that, "There was a little girl/ Who had a little curl/ Right in the middle of her forehead/ And when she was good/ She was very, very good/ And when she was bad/ She was horrid."

Despite the widely accepted idea of Gemini's being of double nature significance, it has little or no bearing upon any tendency towards being bisexual. On the contrary, the men born under Gemini are probably straighter in their sexual proclivities than members of most other Signs. In fact,

43

they "keep their cool" to the point of being about as square as any man can be. In regard to variations and deviations in sexual activity, it would take a lot of persuasion and a great deal of patient teaching to get a Gemini male to indulge either actively or passively.

It is more general in the life pattern of the Gemini male to find a girl and get married—just about as young and as fast as he can. Should this not sound like the conduct of a double personality, which would have internal strife or conflict, the "two" personalities warring with each other, it is not actually inconsistent with the nature of the Gemini male. The reason is that he is very likely to blind the third or inner eye of both his natures and rush into a situation as fast as he can. Why? For a thousand reasons, depending on the complexity of the pattern in his individual chart. Why, in general? Because his cold sex nature wants to change the aloneness of his past experience to the togetherness of the next experience. To him, therefore, marriage satisfies a number of needs; it starts a new cycle of experience which ends the previous one, it is the conventional thing to do, it is something he can regret at leisure, for there is something of the masochist in him. It is an unconscious rushing into pain (of regret, repentance, punishment for having acted swiftly in error), pain which he subsconsciously enjoys.

The influence of the planet Mercury works upon the Sign Gemini in uncharacteristic ways. It is the Ruler of travel and variety, of talk and communications. Gemini is affected and neutral in return. An alluring female who works pretty hard at it can talk a Gemini male into going to bed with her, but she will have to work pretty hard at it. Especially, if she is his peer socially, or if they are members of the same social group. In this event, he is likely to act in a prissy, puritanical way, and be no easy conquest for her. Nor will he be aggressive with any woman under the same circumstances, for convention has too strong a hold on him.

However, the Mercury influence does give him a footloose trait, a desire to travel, to see distant places, to fill his senses with the sights and smells and tastes of romantic ports of call, of the more bohemian sectors of cities at a safe distance from home. In such environments, he lets himself go. What represents danger at home is glamorous adventure abroad. Any one may be sure that adventure includes romance and sex. The adventures are accompanied by much mental pleasure, for this Gemini male's mind never stops working. He is constantly telling himself that this is great, that he is living, that this number is better than the one he had yesterday. He saves up a whole reservoir of memories, and they pay interest in providing erotic experiences in the future and a better understanding of sexual techniques and the quirks of other people.

The outward man of this zodiacal type retains the characteristic Gemini conservatism. He is choosy about his appearance, and his choice is to give the impression of being a right wing Republican, wearing the Brooks Brothers cut no matter how far he lives from Madison Avenue. All his tastes are in line; traditional food, accepted music, classical works of art, and recognized literature. His choice of a lifemate (for however long) will also be conservative and conventional. The lady of his choice must be able to cook and keep house just like his mother. If she looks like his mother, so much the better. If she does not appear on the scene, although he usually finds her, he remains at home with mother.

Where then is the duality of his nature? He wants physical satisfaction, eventually finds it or realizes he can get it. The *but* is within him. *But* what about all the complications? Is that release, the act of sexual joining worth all the complications he has to go through? It can upset his mildly lived conventional existence. It is too much (almost), the same as most thrills or sensations are too much. Or cost too much. Not in money, but in the final effect. Just as smoking, overeating and alcohol will have an ultimate effect, so, feels the Gemini man, will sex have an ultimate effect. Costly to his health, expensive to his peace of mind, deleterious to the pattern of life he has so assiduously and carefully built up.

For all the reasons, whether thought out, understood and/or appreciated, he seeks out a mild woman of appropriate age. She must have and share his tastes in all things. Moderation must be the rule in smoking and drinking, conservatism the rule in dress, thinking, and politics. Neither party to the marriage, by rules, custom, morality, or crystallized habit, may display temper, extremes, or deeply stirring sexual impulses. The reason this mild guy rushes into marriage, most frequently, is the subconscious instinctive realization that he has so much to overcome to enjoy sex that, "Let's get to it." Because he is so big on plans, he feels, more by intuition than self-analysis, that if he keeps building up, it will only be to a letdown. His next stimulus is, "Let's get it over with." If it is a success, it will become a dutiful but not a terribly moving or thrilling habit. Ecstasy? Rare for Gemini.

The dual nature is represented in the pulls to and away from the sex experience. As Gemini is an Air Sign, this element also has an effect on the personality, the hopes and dreams, the way of life of the Gemini individual. He is idealistic, but his hopes may be so impractical that they are or become "up in the air." The Sign endowments are of such

46

a varied and versatile nature that the end results, despite a brilliant mind, can be his doing an ordinary job, be married in a routine family life, and become president of the local Kiwanis club.

Versatility is a gift which needs very concentrated handling, or it means the person so endowed will fritter his talents away by trying to use all of them. The Gemini man could be a great technician in sexuality if he would only concentrate on sex. But he will also be working on a home study course, running a boys' club, conducting a choir, or making travel and vacation plans.

While he knows there are such human diversions as homosexuality, masturbation and oral and anal acts, he mentally stamps them out of existence. All that is exotic seems to be beyond him. The general traits of the Sign do not detract from the potential of sexual attainment and happiness, for the individual birthday as well as the personal chart thankfully provide Nature's variations.

THE GEMINI FEMALE

May 21st to June 20th

As the female member of the Sign Gemini, the woman of the Twins also has complications of personality and desire. There is her strictly mental outlook and her highly idealistic side, but no woman can deny nature, and so there is conflict with the demands of the body. The Aquarian Age, which has brought all occult matters to great popularity, had to include the Woman's Liberation Movement. When the ladies took to the streets, men's bars, and other locations previously set aside for males, the attack was during the Sun's transit through Gemini.

The movement is typical of the Gemini-born female. It is symbolic of the nature of the woman of this Sign, demonstrating and even fighting for some organization or ideal which she considers to be her personal crusade. The power of the Sun's infiltrations into Gemini gives the resemblance of the male and female in their attitudes to sex. The innate coldness makes them matched partners for each other. They would hardly know the fun and joy they were missing in their mutual frigidity.

In appearance, the Gemini-born woman is refined. She has a quality of aristocracy which is a heritage of her Sign plus the seeming withdrawal from all that pertains to sex or is of a sensuous nature. Her looks and expression may seem somewhat autocratic, and if the onlooker gets the impression that she has stepped out of the frame of a portrait done prior to the French Revolution, then the lady is probably a true daughter of Gemini.

Like her male counterpart, the Gemini female has a strong reaction of disgust to any mention of varieties of the sexual act whether with a man or another woman. She is particularly horrified by lesbianism although her attitude towards women's rights is so strong that she may well give the impression of having a man's soul in a woman's body. This is one of the contradictions of the Sign of the Twins, part of the duality of their nature, part of a joke nature played on them. Another trait that may make her appear to be manly is her choice, if any, of male companionship. She chooses the effeminate type of man, not necessarily homosexual, because her impression of him is that he is cleaner or more ordered mentally. She may well get a monster wearing a delicate mask in this way, but she might be really shock-proof by the time she learned of her dilemma.

In line with her superficial dislike of sex, for the variable aspects in the individual chart account for differences, the Gemini-born female takes a long time to make up her mind about getting married. Her inclination is to dilly-dally on this decision. She consciously or unconsciously veers from the physical contact which marriage includes. She steers clear of being touched, played with, caressed, made love to. The thought of the physical agony of giving birth presents a picture of terror to her. This is one experience she will put off as long as possible.

There are many Gemini females who have married. They are intellectual enough to know that married life is the conventional way of living, that it means social acceptance for them, that sex may be a supplementary requirement. But for those advantages marriage offers, they marry. It may be later in life than women born under other stars marry. It will be late in life that they will have children, although they delay this event as long as possible. The maternal instinct is sheltered or suppressed. The lady of the Sign of the Twins would certainly not volunteer gladly to bear children. She does not revere her own mother or mother-hood. Duty may be duty, and bringing up the children is included. However, the Gemini-born mother and her offspring are better off if a nurse or caretaker is in charge of this facet of family life.

The life-long prospects of the Gemini female may seem discouraging to men and women born under the other Signs. To her, however, the limitations of desire do not make her depressed nor discouraged. Her ideals seem so high-minded to her that the sexual aspects of life seem depressing. She may well look forward to an existence devoted to some cause she considers lofty or just or necessary to uplifting mankind, and more especially, womankind.

The Gemini woman may express herself by way of being a poet or a violinist. She would use some descriptive phrase or adjective to distinguish herself as a member of the female sex whether her choice of activity were those mentioned or other areas in the arts or collecting or teaching. It would be in character with her Sign tendencies to have a calling to nursing, to being a working or teaching sister in an order, or even to the ministry in such sects as recognize and ordain female ministers or preachers. Her latter years would bring satisfactions from gardening, caring for a collection of china or painting, or for her pets, which would be substitutes for unmissed male companions. Any woman born under any of the other eleven Signs could not have a better friend when in need, whether that need were for companionship, care, sympathy or cash.

In fact, the female born under Gemini may assume the role of old maid long before her time. In her flight from sex, she may don the appearance of the spinster in movie satires, pulling back her hair into a tight knot, wearing what the hippies now call granny glasses, and generally unsexing her appearance. In this guise, she not only attends the sick and needy among her friends, but is "constant visitor" at the hospital and funeral parlor, consoling, sympathizing and announcing moral precepts and philosophical aphorisms of an "appropriate and correct" type.

While the dominant trait in the mental make-up of the Gemini female is coldness, the physical cannot be forever denied, as has been stated. When aspects cause more heat than thought, the Gemini female can get involved. However, what she is thinking while in the passionate cycle is indicative of the true double-nature of the Sign. For what she is doing is analyzing the man she has decided on. She is measuring in her mind his qualifications as a lover and estimating the size of his sex organ so that she can make her own predictions. She will come pretty close to being accurate in her forecast of the relationship both as to intellectual companionship, social pleasure, and mutual sexual satisfactions to be derived.

One cannot say that such a cool perusal of a potential partner in these three phases of life could lead to great emotional happiness. And it doesn't. Making mental comparisons is certainly not letting one's self go on a spree of enjoyment. Nor does it make the partner feel the sense of security and self-confidence that build his ego and make him a better man in bed. Yet the woman who is doing this to the man has the wisdom of Gemini, the knowledge of how to arouse him, how to tease and excite him into a state of passion and readiness that he may never have experienced with a bed partner born under any other Sign. The negative aspect of this experience is that when it is over, the Gemini woman may barely remember the man's name. She may have explored and caressed the most secret parts of his body with the greatest ardor, yet after she has reached her own zenith of passion and passed it, ask him whether he smokes, or does he drink, or where does he live.

This woman is very complex, and part of this is due to the staying power that she has in the sexual act. While all women escape man's necessity to get ready and can outdistance the male, the Gemini woman really complicates matters in bed by outlasting any male partner.

With her high ideals, the Gemini female lacks many of the truly great aspirations that most lovers cherish in their secret hearts. Expressions of fanciful romance do not come naturally to her lips. And this is strange indeed because in the private chamber of sex, she can use language to arouse her partner that could shock a prostitute in a low-class whore house. One must remember—that is in privacy. But a hike in the woods, a tramp on a boardwalk, even a moon-lit night on board a vessel—these occasions would fail to arouse any tenderness or sweet expression. Indeed, she might react quite severely to any suggestion of an embrace and would surely be angered by one of anything greater. Her nervous system might temporarily go to pieces, and the ensuing scene would be quite exacting.

To avoid unwanted sexual approaches to her, the Gemini woman has an additional dodge to that of a display of nervous hysteria. She has mother. It is to mother that she clings, not father. Mother understands her, protects her, and guides her. She will, if she marries, create a monstrous mother-in-law of her mother, who may well have started out as a nice, plain woman. Given a chance, her Gemini daughter will find a reason to have her mother live with her, whether she is married or single. It is then that she will have the protection that she wants from the world, from what is low-class, from her husband's passionate approaches.

The regrettable aspect of the duality of the Gemini woman is that she is getting the least out of the sadistic-masochistic make-up. She fails to see, despite her mental brilliance, that the masochistic half of her sexual makeup prevents her from letting go in sex, from enjoying it, from trying to reach an emotional and physical outlet that her body was made for. On the other hand, the sadistic half makes her inflict pain or suffering or at the least, refusal of the man who wants to go to bed with her. Neither of these practices results in sex pleasure or real pleasure of an emotional kind. Her duality, which could double her pleasure, denies her any; it denies others any.

Should she wish to ameliorate this condition, she can split her own personality. She has the will power to play the role of one of her two selves, and thus provide a full sex life for herself and endow some man with pleasure.

Cancer: June 21 to July 22

June 21st to July 22nd

The male born under the Sign of Cancer has many joys, many tragedies, and many emotional ups-and-downs in between. He loves love. He requires love. He will go all out for it, and seems to live up to the title of the Restoration comedy about Antony and Cleopatra: *All For Love, Or The World Well Lost.* In seeking to obtain for his own the object of his love, the Cancer male will make efforts unparalleled by any male born under any other Sign.

Because he is so sensitive, however, the man of Cancer needs some encouragement. His sensitivity is quite apparent, and he is very easily hurt. The fear of being rejected plus his innate terrific sense of pride make sexual approaches quite a difficulty. While he is ready in his heart and soul to give his all, he may discover physical and emotional problems that hold him back from attainment or satisfaction. Qualified to be really agressive men in bed, the Cancer males in general comprise the largest number of men who suffer from psychic impotence. The mere idea, soupçon, or suggestion that he is not as wanted as he wants will prevent him from enjoying sexual satisfaction. The love object might just as well throw a pail of ice water on him. In a reciprocal mating in which he does feel his partner is enjoying herself as much as he is, he will express his love, passion, and sexual excitement in sighs, moans, cries, grunts, clutchings, scratchings, and biting. Anyone who reaches a climax or orgasm with him, who has shown as much excitation as he, will be literally a marked woman (or man) for many a day.

All this emoting is but a potential. It is a dynamo which requires some kind of assurance that the relationship contains mutual enjoyment and emotional content. This is because he is so afraid of being used or disdained that he suffers abjectly. Without flattery, encouragement, eternal overt manifestations of affection, he will hide or even bury his most profound desires and wind up in a tragic state of frustration and depression.

The zodiacal symbol of the Sign Cancer illuminates his sexual nature very brightly. It is the Crab, whose claws are the most powerful parts of the entire physical makeup. When the beady eye of the Cancer male (which he is wise enough to disguise in the look he gives the object of his urge) lights upon what he wants, there is an arousal and readiness. The real Crab surrounds its prey with its irresistable pincer, and, snap! What can escape? For whoever tries will only be destroyed.

The Cancer male is a natural playboy, and one who plays the field. He likes sex, and he likes a lot of it with a lot of different people. It can be that his vices are many but that he considers no sexual practice from any but an amoral point of view. His appearance is earthy even though he is a Water

Sign. He gives the impression of a man of passion and lusts, large in physique, light in complexion, fair as to hair. Any woman will see him as a big man, or he can make any woman feel little. Hidden beneath his overt and perhaps practiced gentility is an avid, potent, almost primordial and sexually hungry hunter.

When the Cancer male's claws come together, the object being squeezed will have a full sense of being possessed. This is a figure of speech expressing the great and deep-seated need of the Cancer male for self-realization. With all his sensitivity, he needs to experience a sense of being sufficient unto himself for *now*. It is a clutching at this moment of self-realization that colors both love and sex for him. When the moment, the orgasm, the experience, the *now* has passed, it may turn out to have been literally or figuratively only a moment, in truth. It is the need to *repeat* that moment in order to come alive again that can make the Cancer male wreck his own and his lover's romance. The pattern just described is a very threatening element to the marriage of the Cancer male. Besides being innately sexy all the time, he needs the response of his wife's bodily and sexual reactions to assure him that she is always there for him, that she needs him, too, that she wants him, too, that she belongs to him. Should she not be overly sensual she will have to learn to be the greatest actress on the bed in all the world. She might receive a phone call from London to be in a certain phone booth in Kennedy Airport in New York at a specified time, and to be ready—and already having taken the pill!

This is only one manifestation of the Cancer male's lust. He might also come home a little depressed from too much drinking or having lost at cards. Then he will fall upon his spouse, all care and precaution to the winds and father

58

(another) unwanted child. If she tries to repel him, she will need a lot of the Lord's help. And overcoming her resistance will give him an additional little sadistic lift.

Once this literally "heavy lover" has had his own orgasm with his wife, he is quite unconcerned about whether her unwillingly aroused passions have been satisfied.

The Cancer male is both aware of sex and eager for experience from boyhood. He is curious about "the facts of life," and learns from others what it is about as well as how to masturbate alone and mutually as well as to derive pleasure from other homosexual acts. All this conduct is, however, very sneaky and acted out in secret. Publicly, he is such an avid heterosexual that his whole attitude becomes somewhat offensive. He eventually gets his woman (frequently women), and the older he gets, the younger he likes them. The latter passion can lead to crime, not in his eyes, but in the eyes of the world he feels does not understand his "natural" feelings.

There is an erratic emotional strain in this man which makes him a real American defender of motherhood, home life, children, old people, and pets. He could loose a Niagara of tears at the death of such a one, but not a single one of regret over his own acts of perversion.

The perversity and perversion in his nature are strongly allied to the rulership of his Sign by the Moon. The Moon's other name is Luna, and from it comes the word lunatic which explains the Cancer male's constant or periodic sexual madness. It is said by some that madness verges upon genius, and this accounts for the brilliance of the Cancerian in attaining success in many fields of endeavor, in sexual conquests, and even in covering his tracks after hunting for prey when the Moon is full.

June 21st to July 22nd

The female born under the Sign of Cancer is more womanly than one born under any other Sign of the zodiac. This Sign has a Luminary as its astrological symbol: the Moon. The Moon has an influence on the females born under Cancer even more potent than its unique influence on the Cancer males. The explanation is fairly obvious. The Moon's transit of the natural zodiac is a period of 28 days. In this latter sentence lies the explanation. The first clue is period; the second clue is month. Periodicity, or the monthly, is a phenomenon of nature limited to females. It is inevitable that the lunar month and the woman's period coincide (in "regularity"). The philosophy of pre-destination is not the subject of this analysis. Suffice to say that the teachings of occult philosophy deny that there are any accidents (mere coincidences).

The innate temperament, the changing patterns of behavior of the Cancer-born woman may be attributed to the phases of the Moon. Its influence on their behavior and responses to its vibratory power is greater because they are more sensitive to it. The reaction pattern of lunacy is general during the Full Moon. The Cancer female is constantly reacting. For these considerations the term Moon Children has attained large popularity in contrast to Cancer, which also bears the stigma of being the name of a dreaded disease.

A characteristic of the Cancer female distinguishing her from the Cancer male is her home-loving nature. Also, her desire and search for protection. What Moon power makes the Cancer male a splendid success in extroverted activities makes the female a success in home-making, motherhood, acting the role of the family historian, the reminder of others of anniversaries, birthdays, and other sentimental occasions. In the role of woman, the all-woman Cancerian is very tender, requires and seeks protection, is yearning yet timid, afraid she is unwanted. Changeable as her nature is, for the duration of her passion for "her" man she will be adoring, even from a distance if she can't get closer. Love will be her all-in-all; unrequited, it can quite atomize her personality.

Their reactions in such situations follow a pattern familiar for the many analysts whose couches they are prone to occupy. They take out their frustrations in eating and drinking, turning from escapism into fat depressives. They become subject to tearful drunks, sloppily sentimental crying jags, and evolve into tedious bores. Perhaps the greatest harm they do is to themselves, their showering gifts on their love object and their stupid self-indulgence can make them financially and emotionally bankrupt.

The Cancer girl is home-loving, strongly attached to her parents especially her father. She likes older people, and tends to bring herself to the older male's attention even before she has a full realization of how she might be provoking him nor what the eventual outcome might be. Nevertheless this can work out very beautifully. What started as an unconscious leaning towards an older man can have outcomes very beneficial to both of them. The young Moon maiden seeks the protection of an older man. He in turn is flattered, enjoys showing off to her a little, likes teaching her, and may well fall in love with this nymph and even marry her. She brings joy to his latter years; she can also fully enjoy merry widowhood in well-fixed financial circumstances in return for the pleasure she has given. Should this fairly ideal situation be interruped by her attachment or marriage to a younger man, she will maintain some kind of friendly relationship with her mentor or benefactor, and keep her life that much more replete with satisfactions.

Intrigued by sex early in life, the Cancer girl may experiment. However, her sensitivity plus the individual aspects in her personal horoscope may equally influence her to retain her virginity until she is married. Rebellious if she feels she is an unwanted child, or suffering from sibling envy, she will throw herself into the bed of the first man she can, saying, "Take me." Her resentment against one or both of her parents can make her repeat this until she becomes a fully-experienced, sophisticated woman—at a girl's age. This pattern of behavior has been very common among Cancer girls brought up in too conservative or strict Catholic families. The same is true of rebellious Jewish girls born under Cancer, except that recent manifestations have been their turning hippie and choosing blacks to be their lovers.

These Cancer females give off an aura of sexuality in large measures. The breasts tend to be big and inviting. They are also "a truck driver's idea of a good time" because they give a first impression of being easily available. Blonde or red-headed, more by nature's grace than the hairdresser's artistry, they have a come-hither look, nor do they turn off a man who offers them a drink. Friendly types, they know just how to ingratiate themselves with males of all ages.

Their type is really the father image, but when feeling high, they are not averse to a good healthy encounter with a young stud. Eventually the Cancer female becomes promiscuous like the Cancer male. There is a distinction, however. The male will take or make every possible opportunity to have sex. The female is eclectic. She will not fornicate just for the sake of a party; she likes to know who the male is, talk to him and get to understand him, know his station in life, and above all, feel *safe* with him. This can be any male from a bellhop to her best friend's husband. But she has certain rules she has made up, and she sticks to those rules.

Cancer females develop lines that are good opening shortcuts, and also good closings. A rather well-known red-head who is a true daughter of Cancer has cultivated this methodically. She is frequently approached by men in bars with their cliché introduction. "How about letting me buy a drink for a real red-head?" They don't know when they hear the answer that she is giving it for the thousandth time, "Yes, of course. Thank you. And the collar and cuffs match." These ladies also develop an enticing showgirl walk, a chic way of dressing, and a manner of making men know that at last they have met someone who really understands them.

The life horoscope and outlook for the Cancer female can be very tragic, unless she learns from experience. It is hard for her to believe Ben Franklin's old-fashioned aphorism that experience keeps a dear school, but a fool will learn in no other. When young, attractive, and pursued, the girl assumes this kind of life will go on forever. When married, she thinks she's got a guy for life. When her husband puts his foot down because of her sexual demands which exhaust him, when she drinks too much, or when it becomes obvious she is having extra-marital affairs, she gets shocked, outraged, and thrown out. What a blow! She gets a job, plays around, finds another husband, gets another divorce.

Then panic sets in. She drinks and is promiscuous to get over the panic. If she is lucky, she will revive some old man's potency with her sexual know-how, and be set again for a while. All else lost if her old john goes, she may become a lush, a whore, or turn lesbian. All in the game to her, she says, as long as she's swinging.

The Cancer-born female who does not express the ultimate potential of her Sign characteristics settles down to one husband and many children. Her innate desire is to fulfill nature's only purpose—to reproduce itself. It is mainly when she is thwarted in this that the negative influences of her Sign become fully expressed. Married to an erotic male who thinks she is the zenith of great sex, she will be happy. Married to a rational male of her own Sign, she can find full satisfaction in their mutual desire for fun in and out of bed.

Unfortunately, her coloring will do a lot to undo her. She'll be called a dumb blonde or a hot red-head. Basically, she has a generous nature, and has the potential of becoming a friend in need. She loves antiques, clothes, furs, showy jewelry, cooking and decorating. She is a pal to gay boys and lesbians, and not averse to seeing how you make it with them. Directed by a strong and loving male, she becomes a strong and loving mate or lover. Left to the tide—moving powers of the Moon, she leads a tempestuous and wavy life. For she is truly a child of the inconstant Moon.

Leo: July 23 to August 22

♌

THE LEO MALE

July 23rd to August 22nd

Leo is the Sign of the theatre, of royal kings and of horse-racing. Some understanding of the male born under this Sign leaps to mind from the associations one has. The Leo male considers himself a star, hence desired by everyone. He feels himself a king, and so going to bed with him (if he desires) is a requirement with which he bestows a royal favor upon his partner. And in life's sexual race, the Leo male fully expects to be the winner.

Fair of complexion, ruddy in later years, big and inclined to fat, blue-eyed if typical, the Leo male is a sexually attractive creature. Like male birds, he preens himself; without their beautiful plumage, he bedecks himself in colorful attire in styles a little in advance of the times. He also wears his most alluring smile at all times because he needs people to be attracted to him, to think that he is charming, and he feeds on their society, gestures of friendship, admiration and compliments.

The astrological symbol of Leo is the King of the zodiacal beasts, the Lion. This symbology is an illuminating

67

clue to the sexual nature of the Leo male. It denotes the regal nature of his wooing, and it reveals the way he can be made available himself, by being wooed through flattering him as though he really were a royal personage. He assumes the dominant role in sexual relations. In associations of long standing and in marriage he maintains and acts this part regardless of all the other elements in the partnership. He can be his partner's mental, social and economic inferior, but he is going to wear his Leo crown even in bed if he has to to prove his sexual superiority.

While fine feathers are said to make fine birds, the outward appearance of the Leo male and the high opinion in which he holds himself do not necessarily make him as potent as he would like others to think. He extends himself, in fact, to live up to his claims of sexual prowess. As time goes on, he is likely to overextend himself in this direction and go on to impotence early in life. Debauchery which thus destroys him may turn him on to substitute sexual activities, to variations of debauchery, to perversions, masochism, sadism, or the need for youth, for innocent boys and girls to stimulate his fading powers though he is not really old in years himself.

When he is still at the zenith of his potency, the Leo male still requires the adulation which is the outstanding characteristic of his sexual life. While men of other Signs are more than satisfied to make a sexual conquest or be happy in the mere physical and emotional release of sexuality, the Leo man needs to be told he is marvelous, superb, a stallion, greater than Casanova. There is nothing wrong with this except that he is not aware of the fact that this need reveals some psychic inadequacy. Surely it fails to conceal some minor or major internal strife or emotional unhappiness. The

Freudian school considers the Casanova or Don Juan complex a symptom of suppressed homosexuality. In other words, this Leo male has to keep on repeating sexual acts with women—not to prove to them what a great lover he is—but to prove to himself that he is not a homosexual.

Many stars have been born under the Sign Leo. But many Leo men are actors without ever having been on the stage before the public. Their scene is the drawing room or the bedroom; their stage is the bed. The Leo male can talk his way into the heart of his prospect with brilliance and élan. He can charm, play it cool, play it hot, and if necessary, hypnotize his prospect. What he really wants, and he would be much happier if he knew and understood it, is his prospect to persuade him. But the act goes on, year after year, decade after decade. This glamor boy will be wearing youth's styles when his once athletic form has taken on the shape of middle age; the magnetic smile of youth will hover over wrinkled lips and artificial dentures. But the show must go on.

The Sun, the center of the universe, is the astrological Ruler of the Sign Leo. The sons born while the Sun is in its home Sign also like to be the center of this world, and their world is far more likely to be a big one than a little one. The Leo man is happiest, too, when the Sun returns to his Sign each year. This is the cycle preordained for his personal welfare, for gaining ever greater popularity among women lovers and men friends, for harvesting gifts on his birthday, and for expanding his horizons with his sunny disposition. It is at this time, too, that love blooms and he plucks the prettiest flower from the garden. He will try to keep love fresh, for to his credit, he can love deeply. He will also be a real master, for mastery means ownership, and what he wants is to possess the one he loves.

As the Sun remains steadfast in its eternally held central position, so the Leo male is constant. But in his case, he will remain so only if he has security from his sexual partner, wife, or lover. He makes every effort to establish a plan of life, divided into accurately timed cycles, with precisely planned goals. In his head the life cycle is a time-table. The plans, the goals, and the time-table include his love life and his sex life. In his youth, his schooling is a successful period because he applies himself, and his application extends to after-hours play with girls, leading from fumbling advances to some degree of perfection in the techniques of sex. Those years contain some training in mime, acting, or dancing in amateur performances and lead to a professional career if he has talent which is recognized. He displays a lot of originality, but if he is diverted from an artistic public career, he will apply his talents to some other vocation successfully. Versatility will be both a help and a hindrance, as design, decorating, dressmaking, and other artistic vocations are open to him. He may dabble in several of them, yet eventually turn to an ordinary business to gain the advantage of a steady and reliable income.

There is a typical priggishness attendant upon his early years. Among his siblings and his school friends his set pattern of behavior and his known goals seem a little too much. His choice of sports seems freakish to them, for he likes the no-touch, no-contact type; tennis over football, pingpong over wrestling. It may be this, too, which restrains him from homosexual practices; masturbation over sodomy.

As a fully developed youth, the Leo male will have many opportunities to have sexual experiences. Now, a good looking fellow with a flair for fashion, women and society, he will be sought after. And that is exactly what he likes. He will

70

be sought after by homosexuals, too, and soon learn to turn them off and still maintain their friendship and admiration —all he wants from them. Affairs stimulate him but leave no bruises when they come to an end. Because he has such an innate dislike of what is tawdry, he will choose sexual partners who have grace, charm, and intellect enough to know how to handle the less attractive features of a love affair, its physical aspects, and its end. He is inclined to ignore the "dirty details," and respects a woman who does not impose dates of her monthlies or precautions on him.

While adoring stardom in the world of entertainment, sports, or society, and accepting the adulation of the mob, the Leo male really desires what he considers an ideal marriage. His choice of a wife is going to be a plain woman because he does not want two stars in the same household; the competition for attention would be devastating to his ego. The woman he wants as his lifemate must conform to his own basic principles and personal standards. She should have a plain face, but not be homely, and have good taste in clothes. While he likes to show off his ability as a bartender, he wants his wife to be able to produce excellent meals made by her or under her expert supervision. If motherhood is possible, he wants her to have that attribute as well. In bed he wants her to respond in conventional and normal sexual activity with no imaginative or exotic by-play, side-lines, or freaky novelties.

The Leo male wants children to maintain the family line, to carry on his business, to give status to his social position, and to demonstrate to the rest of the world that he is a potent and normal man. He is also qualified to abide by the rules of the rhythm system approved by the Catholic Church if he is not ready to become a father. It would be neither a hardship nor a painful self-denial for him to have intercourse with his wife on the appointed nights when she was within the "safe" period cycle. His self-restraint and love of rules and time-tables would make him rather proud of his ability to control natural desire and build up to the night when he would join his wife in old-fashioned sexuality by appointment.

July 23rd to August 22nd

Although the Sign Leo is under the astrological rulership of the great Luminary, the Sun, which is the symbol of the male principle, the Leo female is the *sexiest femme* of the women of all Signs. One might justifiably twirl the heavenly circle, the zodiac, and put Leo at the zenith to proclaim the female of that Sign as the living sex symbol.

The Sun's rulership of the Sign does not subtract one iota of femininity from the Leo female. Rather the masculine principle which it symbolizes adds the subtle touch of mystery to her personality which men never seem to understand: that she is subjugating them through her sexual charms—and they never seem to get wise to it!

The lioness, this queen of the sexual jungle, with all her magnetism, hot and searching eyes, exuding the aura and scent of sex, is a cold and calculating sovereign. Her charms make men become infatuated with her on sight, and she is well qualified to lead them up the garden path, and frequently into the potting shed.

Being born while the Sun was in transit through Leo has special significance for the members of this Sign, but especially for the female. She seems to assume a certain luminosity when the Sun returns to the Sign it was in at the time of her birth. Whereas, with a tendency to pale skin and light hair, she may have to avoid exposure or sunburn, she nevertheless develops a summer glow that gives her a look of youthful innocence, no matter what her chronological age. Cleopatra must have had it; she even had Leo as the part of the first syllable of her name.

The subtle mystique of the Leo female is associated with her ability to tell hypnotic tales—lies, in actuality. No other woman is as capable of catching a male like the spider weaving its web as the Leo female weaving a web to catch a man and make him stoop to folly. Nor is it hyperbole that does it nor any other figure of speech. It is pure enchantment. It is a reincarnation of Scheherezade. And how men fall for it!

One trait the world can be sure of in the character of the Leo female is the high price she puts upon herself. This need not be a price tag on a sable coat, diamond ring or anything else on the material plane because she might give herself for kicks in an impulsive moment. But she demands payment in loyalty. Having sex with a Leo woman entails an oath of fealty similar to taking clerical orders or being admitted to the round table. This female may never ask for a glass of water, but she is not incapable of asking one of her lovers to commit murder for her.

In regard to this trait, traditional astrology has always ascribed to her the demand of marriage in exchange for her virginity. Forget it—that may have been the case before the discovery of Pluto in 1930 and the ensuing sexual liberation.

Ask a Leo female under fifty if she was a virgin when she was married. You'll probable get a *yes* answer. Ask one over fifty, and you'll get a laugh for an answer. These were the originators of Women's Lib long before their daughters thought up the idea or the name.

Closely related to the requirement of loyalty as a swap for sex is the Leo female's trait of possessiveness. She has to own her men, if only one at a time. However, she prefers to hold on to them in some way, even after the sex role is played out, or the partner has gotten married, or they're geographically separated. To the Leo female every man she has conquered is like a jewel in her regal necklace. She would feel it was incomplete with any single one missing, lost, strayed or stolen. Her tenacity is great. And, strangely, the partner believes he's on the wrong chain all the rest of his life no matter how good the rest turns out to be.

While she may develop into a sexual firebrand upon maturity, the Leo female does not have any great curiosity in her girlhood days. She may be ambitious if she is interested in having a career, and devote herself to personal progress. But youth means the conventional activities to her of games, school, parties, but not many sports. Born with creative talents, she would rather devote her time to cultivating them than to girl friends or kiddy social life.

The Leo girl develops into a sophisticated young woman through a naturally endowed process of evolution. Because nature is usually generous to her, she has beauty of features, a highly colored complexion, good hair, and a figure that is concave and convex in all the right places with a little extra convex in those places that it counts.

One of her most helpful traits in man-baiting is her wonderful sense of self-adornment. The Leo female can embellish what nature gave her with great style. The cosmetic art is inborn, and the Leo woman can be daring in dress, but more important, she has a dramatic sense about the way she looks. She can make an entrance that will make every man in the room want to possess her and make every woman hate her because of jealousy.

Beneath this chic, dramatic, and sophisticated exterior there is an impulsiveness already briefly noted, but important enough to be expanded upon for a complete understanding of the Leo female. She has great self-control when she has a specific goal in mind in her dealings with a man. This may range from business to marriage. Where neither is involved, she gladly abandons that control, or the internal combustion just sets her on fire and she can let go and have great sexual pleasure because she has to have that sensation right at that minute. Gone are her conventional controls. Gone is the psychological censor. She, too, is gone—gone on a male because he has big muscles or a big build, or big genitals. Then the haystack is as good as the Ritz, the self-service elevator is Eden, or the back of a hack is her swan bed.

Outside of these impulsive—compulsive sexual adventures, one might get the impression that the Leo female is an over-serious type. This is the wrong impression, for the lady is funny and fun to be with as well as fun in bed. Leo rules the theatre, and this female goes for laughs as well as for dramatic entrances. She has wit, originality, and such powerful self-confidence that she exudes an air of untroubled lack of concern about the usual petty worries that upset individuals and harry the world.

An unexpected trait in this gal is a hidden sentimental streak. She aspires to practically a royal marriage, but the male she was intimate with holds an unforgettable place in her computer mind. The information retrieval center of her memory is full, and she can continue an association with a former bedmate until her dying day. The fealty and loyalty she demands of every sex mate she, too, has for him. Called on for help from an old lover, she responds. And with her penchant for the royal way, she is likely to say, *Noblesse oblige* as she reaches for her check book to help out some partner she may have made it with years ago in her past.

Sex is also a way of receiving homage, flattery, affection, and satisfaction for their innate exhibitionism and puffed-up egos. It is the applause some Leo females get only in the bedroom, as so many other Leo gals get it on the stage (plus in the bedroom). These seemingly extroverted ladies also suffer badly from rejection or blighted romances. However, all being actresses, professional or non, they hide their emotional burdens.

The Leo female will never let go of sex or her hold on men through sex. The scintillating females wearing wigs and diamonds in jet set cafés are old Leo girls—never letting go of their concept of themselves as stars. And why not? They are stars, every last one of them, until the last glimmer goes out.

Virgo: August 23 to September 22

August 23rd to September 22nd

To avoid confusion about the rulership of both Gemini and Virgo by the same Planet, Mercury, some clarification is made. Gemini is an Air Sign. Virgo is an Earth Sign. As the ruler of each, Mercury displays a different temperament and influence according to the nature of the Sign. As the ruler of Gemini, its influence is fluffy rather than solid. Its subject, the Geminian, is intellectual, but his interests are not profound topics or areas of discussion or study. As the ruler of Virgo, its influence is earthy in the Earth Sign. Its power makes its astrological subject more "down-to-earth" with, although similarly intellectual, a deeper interest in achievements on the material plane.

The symbo of the Sign Virgo is not one of the zodiacal beasts. It is the Virgin, and the symbol, of course, applies to both the males and females born while the Sun is transiting Virgo. Here the symbology applies to the nature of the Virgo male—no matter how exciting his sex life may be. His attitude and mental approach to sex are virginal. His original state is virginal. To him the religious concept of having been born in or of original sin is a farce. His mental set or simplex is his original virginity. How he soils this purity may give him thrills and kicks, even the pain-pleasure syndrome of sado-masochistic perversion, but to him all these are accidents, for there he is a virgin forever.

The Virgo male presents a picture of utter respectability to his world, and because of his intellectuality and prosperity, frequently to the larger world. The emphasis he places upon old-fashioned morality naturally makes him call attention to himself in a permissive world, one which has generally lost its moral standards to the extent of legalizing abortion and homosexuality. His ability to concentrate can lead him to attaining fame in any number of areas of scholarly endeavor, research, and original invention and composition.

The Virgo male is an even greater connoisseur and critic than those Gemini males also ruled by Mercury. He may be a greater research scholar or investigator and critic than original creator because he has a special talent for observation. Let it be said in his favor, he will be equally efficient at finding items to praise as well as to condemn. This proclivity extends to his sexual activity. Once in bed with a partner, he may analyze her (or him) right to his inner core. It may be that this analytical trend is also a subconscious transfer of guilt. By this process, he can really subtract all self-analysis from his cerebral processes and transfer the entire sexual mating to the activity of his partner. The remainder in this little arithmetical game will be his own virtue. Conclusion: he has regained his virginity as a member of the Sign Virgo.

The extension of the influence of the mind over his sexual activities may be so long and strong that the typical

Virgo male, directed by the solar energy in his chart, may restrict his associations with girls to mental or mere social relationships. The word girl is used intentionally because the Virgo male is far more attracted to people younger than he is, especially females. His incisive mind finds too much to criticize adversely in people his age or older. While he is a stickler for convention, he may not recognize this trait within himself and deplore it in others. The fresh loveliness of youth appeals to him. It also gives him the opportunity to display his own erudition; he is pedantic, and loves to show off his own knowledge as well as to take the young under his tutelage and teach them. That middle-aged professor who married one of his students, half his age, was doubtless a Virgo. And the child bride became a fine scholar, but probably not in bed, for there the husband may have had the same innocence as the bride.

The whole attitude of the Virgo male towards marriage is unique. He has no innate physical cause for refraining from a full and joyous sex life. He simply thinks that to give in to the demands of the body shows lack of control of it. And control of the body through the mind is one of the standards and ideals that the Virgo man insists upon maintaining. This man is indeed unfortunate if he fails to analyze his bride-to-be with his usual acumen, for he may become tied to a sensual young female. Then hell would surely replace the expected heavenly bliss. What a tragic discovery it would also be for a young girl hoping to be deflowered and thrilled by an older, experienced man. Should the man be prominent and the marriage the object of newspaper stories, the predictions that "it won't last" might soon come true. If a compromise is made to satisfy the young woman, psychic impotence may ensue because that censor in the Virgo's head will not stop working. He will make himself impotent to avoid doing something that will dirty even his legal marriage.

The rulership of Virgo by Mercury fails to endow this zodiacal type with great masculinity or good looks. Yet he chooses attractive women because he is intellectually eclectic, but is equally satisfied if he fails in this pursuit, with a plainer Jane. It is not statistically inevitable that more Virgo males remain unmarried, but it is likely. The simpler women, chosen by a Virgo not overly interested in sex, will be glad to have a mate, to learn from him, to share in his reflected (intellectual) light.

The ability to analyze others leads the Virgo male to the trait of over-developed curiosity, normal curiosity being a human trait shared by all Signs and both sexes. Fair judgment may not always be the outcome of a bigoted mind, and the Virgo mind, while clever, especially at finding flaws, may pronounce sentence in a highly prejudicial fashion. It is in sexual matters that this becomes an issue. It can lead but to the grave of sentiment, of true feeling, of empathy, and sexual virility.

It is the negative nature of the analytical side of the Virgo male that is pathetic. If all the efforts were the satisfaction of his curiosity and result in a deep-seated emotional satisfaction, one might cheer him on. But when it is to be observed that so much misdirected force fails to stimulate, to arouse, to progress to a never-to-be forgotten romance, good! But to find out what is under a woman's skirt by lifting it and then dropping it can only be considered a frustrating exercise in futility. And one would have to get inside the chambers of this Virgo male's mind to learn definitely whether he knows it is frustrating!

On the positive side of his analytical nature, the Virgo male is qualified to pick a lover, mate, or spouse with whom he can share affection and sexual intercourse. He has sufficient passion where trust is mutual, to more than muddle through, and this is honestly intensified by his loyalty and her willingness to cooperate in bed as well as to be a real helpmate in the attainment of his personal aim in life.

Divorce is not uncommon in the Virgo male's life. He is easily discouraged by his wife's illnesses or pregnancy and flees to the courts for relief. This in no way, however, subtracts from his loyalty to his children if any. He is also moody, and during the few cycles in his life when romantically aroused, he will really do something direct and positive. Because he is a warm soul, being left will not alter his essential nature nor his equanimity.

There are outlets for his nature that surpass sex, and he will go to some lengths to reach them. He can be a big spender, but also be one on borrowed money. As a host, he can be more generous than his pocket actually can afford. Yet in some way, the guest will pay a price for the hospitality he has received.

This man can be witty and magnetic when he wants to put himself out. Yet with old friends, and those with whom he shares confidences, he can be dour and depressing. Later life may well find him wondering where his youth has gone and whether he has not wasted it.

August 23rd to September 22nd

The rulership of the planet Mercury over the female born under the Sign of Virgo is a more congenial factor in her life than it is ever likely to be in the life of the Virgo male. The feminine nature attunes more easily to the changeable nature of Mercury's influence, and the mercurial nature of the planet is in deeper coordination with the influence of the Moon which rules the female than it is with the Sun which rules the male.

The Moon's influence universally makes the female what she is; a physical being responsive to its natural cycles. Mercury enhances or at least increases the changeable nature of the female born under its reign. Mercury makes the Virgo woman more talkative, more flighty, more temperamental, more taciturn. It also gives her more magnetism and greater eloquence than the Virgo male, and takes away none of the intellectual power it endows upon him. One might say that Mercury gives the daughters a better break than it does the sons of Virgo.

The versatility of the Virgo woman manifests itself in a variety of activities. In the first place, her love of learning makes her more or less a perpetual student. She also loves to display her erudition. This female shares the outstanding trait of curiosity with the Virgo male. In her reaching for knowledge, she will attract and use men for her own end, and rarely for their benefit. She can have an encyclopedic knowledge of sex in its every aspect. Whether this knowledge ever leads to sex, better sex, or more sex will depend upon the moment of her birth and the aspects in the heavens at the time. A typical daughter of Virgo, however, will have such affinity for the symbol of her Sign, the Virgin, that it would take far more than knowledge—even of the joys of sex—to persuade her to lose the security her virginity gives her.

Security is not the only factor in the situation. Pride plays a great part in the conduct of her life. She takes inordinate pride in her parents, and remains a little girl in many ways for many years. She calls her parents by the endearing names of her childhood until both she and her parents are old people. Momsy and Popsy can be her great loves until she is long past becoming a mother herself.

The earthy quality of the Sign Virgo has much to do with the formation of her character although less of its sexual side than is normal, satisfactory, or rewarding. Aside from the sexual side, the Virgo female is generally healthy, big, a good eater, and inclined to be a big drinker once she discovers that alcohol (temporarily) kills her inhibitions. Being intelligent, she will cope with the effects of overeating and over-drinking, diet, visit psychiatrists, conquer, and then fall back.

The overdoing due to the earthy influence of her Sign will eventually make her a liberated female, but not necessarily a happy one. She is vengeful, and will turn on a loved one for some imagined slight, jealousy, or because her emotions have been poisoned by a vicious so-called friend. These motives can lead to breaking a relationship, divorce, and becoming a lesbian or allowing a lesbian to dominate her life, her career, and her total sexual expression.

With her notions of virginity, the Virgo female does not strive to be the plate of fashion. Her imagination fails to stimulate her to enhance such sex appeal as she might have because predominant in her psyche is the presentation to the world of the virgin image. Painters have portrayed the Virgin for centuries as a beautiful but sexless woman. The classic portraits make one wonder how they could bear a child or even experience the virgin birth. This is the limitation of the Virgo woman in her own mind. Because she is a female, however, the innate endowments of womanhood, grace, and charm are there.

A clever man, one with personal magnetism and a special kind of sex appeal, could make a real woman of the Virgo female. With one exception: that man could never be a Virgo male. A marriage between a Virgo male and a Virgo female leaves no room for the necessary negative-positive elements that make for magnetic attraction. How can a high-minded person be made more high-minded? Only emotional, intellectual and sexual sterility could result.

When the Virgo female marries a male born under another Sign, many types of relationships are possible. With all eleven potentials, she has a natural tendency to choose the weakest specimens. Her search for a man means a search for a man she can dominate. Forever uplifting, she will seek a male she can feel she is raising to a higher mental, moral, and spiritual plane. If she ever gets to have sex with him, and it is a possibility, she will devour him in all these three senses like the insect which devours the male immediately after copulation. After all, hasn't he served his only purpose? Then, too, with a penchant for younger men she rationalizes her feelings as motherly. Here there is danger, too, for she might then be like the animal that eats its young.

It is difficult for the Virgo female to maintain ordinary relationships with other people. In sex, she wants to dominate. In friendship she finds it difficult to refrain from criticizing. In business, her ambition and executive ability make her hard to work with, harder to work for. None of this detracts from her innate ability.

The influence of Mercury predominates the life of the Virgo female. In addition to illuminating her mind and critical capacities, it gives her eloquence which aids her in persuading the men in her life to do her will. These efforts are typically to uplift them in some way, and atypically to do her bidding in sexual acts. Although her inclinations towards sex are repressed, she has cycles and emotional stresses that do require physical expression, and then she can talk any man she wants into—her! This talkability can work in reverse, too, for she can produce such a Niagara of words, manifest such a case of logorrhea that she can also talk herself out of anything. She tends to hyperbole when stimulated by alcohol, a man, or an audience—or the combination of any two or all three. Here is where she meets her downfall in sexual play. The mouth will go on and on, but not where it is going to arouse any erogenous zone in the male. His mind may have begun by being stimulated, but soon all symptoms of male stimulation have been talked down.

Theory and experience are two different things, and in the life-span of the Virgo female they may be far apart. The Virgo girl finds out a lot about sex because she asks questions. She goes on asking them until she has a vast storehouse of knowledge. Because all information becomes a part of her mental retrieval system, she does not shock easily. However, she is not one to rush into a man's arms or bed to try out what she knows.

The only time she combines theory and knowledge is when she has sex with her husband. By the time the Virgo female marries, she knows it all. She decides to have a child, and she certainly will not have one by accident. Then all the biological information she has gathered comes into play. Timing, position, etc., will go into the mating that is to result in conception. This will be followed by diet and exercise. This kind of sexuality may impress one as terribly calculated, so much so that it would seem there could be little excitment, no imagination, and hardly any passion in the act. And that's just about how it would be—a cold, calculated intimacy.

The Mercury influence has another effect on the Virgo female. It makes her restless. When transiting the Fifth House of her chart, Capricorn, the lady will pack her bag, pick herself up, and travel to almost anyplace that comes to mind. She may announce it's for a rest, recuperation, or study. It's really an answer to the call to satisfy her curiosity about some new place and the men and women she can find there.

Many are the facets of the nature of this changeable female. Depending on the aspects in their birth charts, of *all* Virgoans, one will find them flirtatious, driving men mad by never giving in. Others will give the impression they are leading to the bed by asking questions. In fact, they only want to know the answers. Rare, but around, is the eccentric one. She will insist that everything about her and around her be unconventional. Shock is her weapon of subduing. Liquor is the outlet for another variety in the Virgo garden. This female will drink herself into bed or talk herself out of it. Lastly is the Virgo female who wants her brother or her father or a woman. This is the one to beware of. She is the original "more deadly than the male."

illustrations

Hebe, Greek goddess of youth

Aphrodite, Greek goddess of love and beauty

Amazon warrior

Two loving couples, (Greek vase)

Erotic wall fresco of Pompeii

Renaissance drawing depicting romantic love

16th century concept of man as the center of all
things

Dante's lovers.

17th century concept of ideal male and female
bodies.

Indian temple sculpture

18th century drawing depicting an orgy

The Lovers, Jean Fragonard

Lovers, (drawing c. 1784)

Lovers, Paul Gauguin

The Lovers, J.L. Gericault

Rape, Francisco de Goya

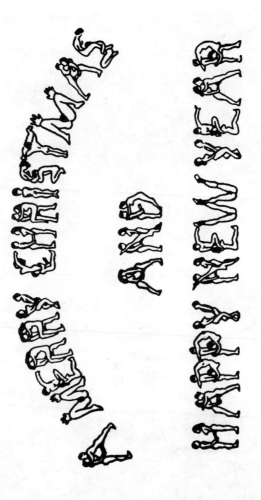

English greeting card (c. 1890)

Lovers, Gustave Doré

The Kiss, Auguste Rodin

Libra: September 23 to October 23

THE LIBRA MALE

September 23rd to October 23rd

The Libra male is a sex-ridden love-mad man as the planetary ruler of his Sign is Venus, as it is for Taurus. The difference between the influence of Venus on Taurus and Venus on Libra is the position of "the morning and the evening star," in the natural zodiac. The Libra male has an intuitive awareness of absolutely everything related to sex: its physiological, emotional, and psychological contents. He has a profoundly intuitive understanding of normal and abnormal sexuality, and he increases this knowledge with information culled from study, observation, and experimentation. Almost the antithesis of his zodiacal next door neighbor, Virgo, he sees nothing but the joy of living in hot, raging, unthinking copulation. While the Virgo male is busy reforming (in the worst sense), the Libra male is busy converting. He is trying to get the whole world to see, feel, taste, smell, and endure the heat of the contact of two bodies joined and convulsed in the act of love. Nor would he mind if that whole world were a populace of his lovers—all his.

113

The variance in the effect of Venus on Taurus and Libra is also the outcome of the nature of each Sign. Taurus is an Earth Sign, and makes the Bull such an appropriate symbol for it. Libra is an Air Sign, and we therefore find Venus floating rather than earth-bound. The effect of this difference on the Libra male is to make him light-hearted, mobile, airy (although subtle) in his sexual relations, and happy-go-lucky in contrast with the similarly Venus-ruled Taurus.

Venus is the goddess of beauty; the planet named after her rules not only over beauty of the body, but beauty of the mind and its most artistic and ravishing creations. In this case, creations refer to all the products of the creative mind: poetry, painting, sculpture—the lively arts, in other words. Bringing this figurative language down to the material plane gives us the interpretation of the Libra male's love of beauty, in all forms. But primarily in the form of a beautiful, sexy, luscious, delicious, stimulating, almost (and sometimes) edible sexual partner—boy or girl.

The symbol of the Sign Libra is the Scales. This is the only Sign of the zodiac which has neither a beast nor a human as its symbol, another indication of the unique character of the Sign. The symbol stands for human characteristics, some of the noblest ones that can be attributed to mankind. They are in fact ideals, such as justice, symbolized by balance, plus the noble qualities which accompany it. The balance is represented in the male in his integrity and sense of fair play; in his creative efforts in the correspondences of his art; in his philosophy in the ying and the yang.

Fortunate is the woman who captures a Libra male. Fortunate is the Libra male, for destiny endows upon him the physical qualities of good looks, a magnetic personality, a shining pair of eyes, height above average, a swinging gait, and magnificent presence. Truly he is at least a minor hero, a movie hero, and a hero to his own world. Nor does fortune frown upon him nor despoil his looks until a very advanced age, whereupon he learns that the personality traits garner for him as many hearts as once his physique alone did. Nor are the members of his sex fan club his chronological peers nor opposite sex, for girls and boys, and men and women find him magnetic right up to the end.

The symbolic Scales of his Sign give the Libra man a great sense of balance in the world where he conducts his life including the sexual side. This lover might have a dozen mistresses, but he manages to keep everything cool. It would be rare for him to be involved in a scandal because he knows how to conduct himself, his business, his family affairs in the conventional world. Realizing the pitfalls beneath the cliff, he manages to hold on to his equilibrium, maintaining almost magically all the burdens he must balance in any precarious position.

Love is a prime requisite to the happiness of the Libra male. As easy as he finds sexual conquest, he feels it a rather hollow experience unless accompanied by a deeper emotion than mere orgasm arouses. While deeply moved at the moment of joining, he subsequently experiences a kind of letdown. He might question its value, its truth, its honor, its effect. There might be an element of gratitude, but what he is being grateful for is more for having been loved for a glorious moment than merely for the sexual experience. This is part of the complexity of the Libra male's makeup. It is his heritage to cause others to fall in love with him, but conscious as he is of his own profound and moving charms,

115

somewhere deeper within him is a need for reassurance. The sex partner who hands out the biggest dose of attention, who lays on flattery with a trowel, is the one who will be rewarded in turn by passionate love making.

With all his idealism and romantic nature, the Libra male has a physical side which becomes more evident as he grows with experience. The seeming eternal youth may go on making the façade almost beautiful and seemingly naive year after year. But the sexual nature does become a little jaded. No one can really live on a diet of rich foods exclusively. So the beautiful boy meets girl and they have beautiful sex; this can develop into a sophisticated boy meets girl and suggests little experiments that will bring variety into the beautiful sex. And variety is widely known to be the spice of life.

Such attractive men can generally succeed in introducing variations in their love-making. It adds not only to the sensual pleasure of the sex performances, but bolsters the ego of the Libra male to have his partner accede to performing acts that might be just a little (or more than) bizarre. Judged by his entire performance in sex, the Libra male might be found just a little wanting. His ego can be so exaggerated by successes that he concentrates only on his own satisfaction. While this might leave some of his partners unfulfilled, some might be so enthralled at having him at all in the flesh that they learn a new kind of kick—a masochistic pleasure in the service of an idol. It should be said that if the Women's Lib movement is ever put down, it will be put down by a group of organized Libra males. They would know just what to do to make the liberated women cringe, give up, and finally plead to be allowed to be real women—men's women—again.

The Libra male's sexual growth starts early in his life.

His looks and/or his magnetic sweetness combined with his sexual aura make him the object of the pursuit of his school mates, young women, older women, and sybaritic homosexuals. He soon learns the joys of intercourse, and excess may become his success. With a person who is not held back by moral or religious scruples or repressions, he has a great time and becomes a master of scientific sexology.

Marriage can be a splendid experience for the Libra male provided his spouse is free-wheeling. It is doubtful that marriage with any other kind of women would last. She would have to love him deeply, tell him so, and show him by being everything he could want her to be.

The marriage with the chosen and lucky lady is usually a little later in his life than the age other Sign members marry. He wisely waits until his wild oats have been sown—and sow them he must. Having left despoiled virgins, willing older partners, and a lot of broken hearts behind, he marries a grand woman, and goes on having women fall in love with him. Then he goes on his amoral way unless his mate is keeping him at home with the practice of her art of love.

Here is a male who has a wonderful destiny. Fortune has favored him by designing his birth while the Sun is in Libra. He is a man's man in business, social, athletic life. He is a woman's man, almost every woman's man, in the bedroom.

September 23rd to October 23rd

Venus rules Libra just as it does Taurus. What applies to the Libra male applies to the Libra female, i.e., the effect of Venus on Libra is different from its influence on Taurus. In the Libra female, an Air Sign woman, Venus's influence can be seen in her innate grace and charm, in her truthfulness, sense of honor, and the symmetry or rational balance she seeks in life—to live up to the ideal expressed in the symbol of her Sign, the Scales.

While Venus is the goddess of love in mythology, the inference extends to the influence of the planet Venus which is the astrological ruler of love. This is reputed to be a symbol of good luck, although there are dozens of cynical definitions of that emotion. However, in astrology, Venus is known as "the Lesser Fortune"—bringer of life's good things, Jupiter being "the Greater Fortune." Venus's gifts are not, as Jupiter's are, on the material plane. Venus brings to the Air Sign Libra female love, idealism in her emotional relationships and outlook, and a love of all things beautiful— those of mind, the arts, and the heart.

The Libra female makes an idol of the person she loves. In her lover she finds the stimulus to try her best to do all she does perfectly. The idol is her inspiration and the object of her adoration. If "love makes the world go 'round," it puts the Libra female into orbit. There is nothing on earth or in heaven she will not do for her beloved. She is born with great personal magnetism, but the words and actions that come from her when she first sees the object of her love can become almost hypnotic. And "whoever loved that loved not at first sight?"

The Libra female is a real woman. In today's world that is a rare human being. One would hardly find her in a Woman's Lib movement or parade, for what she wants at most is equality, not superiority. She does not crave the use of men's bars, nor men's toilets. The typical Libra Lady, as Birdfeather, the young generation's leading astrologer is known, is good to gaze upon, well-formed, taller than most, thin but with magnificent arms, hands and legs. Everything is in its proper place, well proportioned, and all the parts move with grace. Her gait is sexy and attracts attention. She is born to public life as much as is the child of Leo, and usually finds her way into the spotlight in a vocation connected with or in the theatre, modeling, television, or public office.

Early in life, the Libra female learns all about sex. She has a fine mind, and those secrets that are kept by her parents and teachers soon become simple facts of life to her. While she has great acumen, her knowledge of life is so intimate that she will not find fault with those whose tastes differ from hers, even in sexual matters. The young Libra female learns not only from friends and books, but from life itself. Because she sees nothing denigrating in any form of sex, she neither criticizes others nor finds it impossible within herself to experiment. She may well be sleeping around even in her teens, with boys or girls, feeling her way to some final decision as to what she really wants out of the sexual experience. It is to be doubted that these experiences lack emotional content. That would be atypical of the Libra Lady. Tenderness would surely be present whatever else might be absent from the mating.

The springboard for sex in the Libra female is, indeed, in the romantic ideals with which she is born. Women of Scorpio and Pisces, for example, among other Signs, start with sex and find love. Not so the Libra female. The Libra lady seeks love and then learns to love sex. Another trait, though not as evident, is the ability of the Libra female to view and judge her sex drive and experiences very intellectually. With her innate sense of balance (the Scales), she is a woman who can control the drive with her will power.

The taste of the Libra female runs to men of her own nature. She prefers a man who is all male in appearance as she is all woman in appearance. Self-confidence and a liking to show off without conceit are also traits in the sex partners that attract her. The man who exhibits his masculinity and has a dash of exhibitionism appeals to her. She is like that herself and finds these characteristics admirable. For this reason she can find the best of lovers or a mate among the males of her own Sign, Libra. Indeed such a marriage would be ideal, for therein lies the perfect match and the precise balance of the Scales.

Her good taste extends to her surroundings. With the Venus influence so strong in her horoscope, she is qualified to create beauty in her aura. She can find the best clothing, if necessary, at the best price, and she has a knack of decorating her home economically but in a way that conceals economy and is most impressive.

Venus endows loveliness upon the Libra female. More than any other Sign members, she seems to be the living example of Shakespeare's description of Cleopatra, "Age cannot wither, nor custom stale, her infinite variety." She passes from decade to decade of her life cycle seemingly unchanged. With this preserved youth, so skilfully aided by charm and chic, she retains her sex appeal into the late years. She might well recall her lovers in old age as did the greatest of French courtesans, Mme de Maintenon, "I was barely seventy then."

One of her greatest charms is the spell she seems to cast because of the mystery she makes of love. This lady can perform the most erotic sexual acts without a blush. In apparently the greatest of dignity, there would be neither shame nor hesitation. It would seem rather that she was performing some sacred ritual, so profound, so arcane that it must never be mentioned!

In such matings there must be an equal understanding that all the rites of love are holy. There must be a safe and congenial temple of romance. It must be sterilized clean, but mirrors, candles, hangings of love scenes, and incense would be splendid and erotic additions. Then after the cooings and murmurings, the whispered avowals, the high priestess of love commences her sacerdotal mass.

If the partner in this ritual lacks imagination, stamina, or potency, there will be great disappointment in store for both. The Libra Lady will soon dismiss her partner and an acolyte will be found, for she cannot live without love. Perhaps less without love than without sex. Should this entire process be delayed by negative aspects in the personal horoscope of the Libra female, one must not think it is either hopeless nor that it leads to depressing frustration. She's a smart female. She will wait, plan, campaign, and win. This patience is evinced as a very strong trait. It shows not only in love affairs, but in other important ways in the conduct of her life; at home, in business, and in the general course of events, in marriage. Tolerance is a partner to her patience. Only if either or both are stretched too far will the elastic break. But an elastic makes no explosion, and neither will the Libra female. She will quietly vanish into the effluvia where her own peace of mind and self-control remain in complete charge of the conduct of her life.

To the Libra female love and sex act as a dynamo of unleashed power. These elements are like the forces of a raging river; in their natural state they are an awesome and magnificent sight. Leashed by a brilliant mind, they store up electrical energy that creates the type, the Libra female, who can easily become the queen of her own world.

Scorpio: October 24 to November 22

THE SCORPIO MALE

October 24th to November 23rd

The Scorpio male is one of the strangest, most magnetic, and sex-mad of humans. He is born under the Sign of a unique "beast" of the zodiac, the Scorpion. This creature of nature is symbolic of wisdom and power, both traits of the Scorpio male. He is a passionate and potent man, always interested in sex, constantly on the prowl, and very successful in getting what he wants.

There is a charismatic quality to the Scorpio male's personality which makes him the love object of people of both sexes. This quality is also in evidence in his business and social life. He seems to make other people feel better, have more confidence in themselves. This mystique can become a nuisance to him because the weaklings of the world seek him and want to lean on him, to use his strength. The same applies to those who want to experience sex with him. They, too, will try to lean on him, drain his stamina, live off him physically, spiritually, and financially.

The Scorpio male learns about sex at such an early age that one might be led to think he was born knowing all about it. He has early homosexual experiences, for in many cases his father will find him irresistible and his brothers will be in love with him. He has ancient wisdom, and is, as the occultists say, an old soul. There is some dream-like state he attains in childhood while having actual adult sex experiences. He seems to understand the entire procedure, and to accept it wordlessly. Later in life, he looks back upon these childhood experiences with understanding and sympathy. There is nothing for him to forgive because he has never considered what he or the others did wrong in any sense of the word. It is as though he knew it had to happen because it was meant to happen. Actually this is a part of the ancient wisdom which is also a part of his natal heritage as a son of Scorpio.

Because of his high native intelligence, the Scorpio male is a leader in the activities in which he participates, including the sexual experience. He has a great deal of will power and more self-control than is visible on the surface. Because he loves fun and games and the sport of sex, he seems to be so frivolous that there might not be any strength beneath the gay exterior. Far from it! He has control, can resist temptation if he wants to, and is a dynamo of power when he is enjoying the sexual experience.

Scorpio is a Water Sign, and the male of the clan is a potential alcoholic, only provided he enjoys drinking, and with the realization that he has sufficient strength of will and self-control to quit whenever he wants to. This trait may easily give the appearance of stubborness, and one must not be misled by the sweet impression he gives. He can be stubborn, and persuasion will be useless. Only his own inner motives ever sway the Scorpio male.

The Scorpio male is a great attraction to women and

to homosexual men. His allure, his gait, his looks, all act as magnets. He himself, with all the self-control described above, shows little emotion, and the secret is that he is really more concerned with himself than with anyone else. In truth and in fact other people are not necessary to him. He can always and easily find someone to have sex with. He does it as one plays a game. The release leaves him perfectly contented, and he can part from his lover's bed with no emotion, romantic illusions, or sentimental hangovers.

On the other hand, no one can really hurt the Scorpio male but himself. He may make enemies, not through useful acts really, but through negligence or acts of omission. But within himself there lies a hidden enemy. It is the desire for sensation. He can control himself, it has been said, but when he desires an experience he will go all out to have it, with his eyes open. And with no regrets or guilt following it; this he knows in advance. What, then, can happen? Overindulgence. He can go all out for alcohol or for stimulants in the mood-changing drug family, or hard drugs, and he has the potential of becoming a devotee of the psychedelic drugs.

There is a tremendous affinity with the world of the occult. To open the doors of it, the Scorpio male is willing to try anything. Pot, mescaline, LSD, all these and their kindred varieties do not frighten him. He will try them on for size, fearlessly. If the results bring the desired effects, or if he enjoys them, he will repeat the experience. If the sensation does not bring satisfactions, he will add it up to the list of life's nothings, forget it, and never return to it.

The effect of the Scorpio male on his sexual prey can be emotionally fatal. The symbol of the Sign, the Scorpion, represents the death-dealing sting of this unusual "beast." The Scorpio male can inflict such a sting on his sexual victim in a way to render the partner numbed with conflicts, strifes, internal wars, and suicidal depression. It is doubtful that a member of any other Sign group has such tremendous power and influence. The strange thing about it is that it is an unconscious natural force. It is like lightning in that it does not know its own strength, yet it is a strength which can kill with one strike. A partner in sex of the Scorpio male will never forget him, and forever after make comparisons, mostly odious.

The reason is that the Scorpio male develops techniques of love that can drive his partner to sensual insanity. He has no sense of shame. On the other hand, he is conscious of his body at all times. He uses it in the whole and in all its parts like a wonderful bow, with his partner the violin. The music he evokes is like a threnody, for he calls forth every possible vibration until the two partners reach such a state of ecstasy that they may well be hearing "the music of the spheres."

This man will leave no cell unknown or untouched. He can start at the feet, for like Pisceans he has a love of them, worshiping from the toes up and the head down. He will evoke unnerving, shattering, and unforgettable sensations. And the entire act will affect him like some powerful narcotic. He will also have sensations that take him into a realm like never-never land!

Classical good looks are not typical of the Scorpio male. He looks rather unfinished in some way—a statue that the sculptor has not smoothed but whose effects are greater and sexier for that reason. He dresses in an attractively careless way, and this informality only adds to the charm he already exudes.

The woman who marries a Scorpio male can expect

much philandering. He will avoid becoming a father if he can. But he will take his beloved dog out for long walks, and while he is gone, he will be busy, looking and flirting, and if successful, sneaking in a short affair on the side.

Promiscuity is a way of life, not an immoral way to his mind. The more (sex), the merrier. For this reason, he carries on for the experience, the sensation, and this leads him to enjoy sex with both men and women in every possible way, any "degenerate" act being not only acceptable but deeply enjoyable. The exclusively homosexual Scorpio male is the most promiscuous of all Signs, for there are hardly enough partners around to keep him happily occupied. He also likes a dash of bitters: if his trade has some disfigurement he would say of him, "That is sensual."

THE SCORPIO FEMALE

October 24th to November 22nd

Intense and permanent desire for sex characterizes the true Scorpio female. Her Sign is under the astrological rulership of Pluto, the most mysterious and distant of the known planets. Not as much is known about the influence of Pluto as about other planets because it was discovered only comparatively recently. Its existence was known; its discovery revealed the reasons for many unaccounted for past events. This is brought out because there is some similarity to the strange behavior of the Scorpio female. She is always ready for sex, yet she does not indulge herself in the satisfaction of her desires. Her motives are the mystery; she may not even be able to analyze them herself.

Yet the "mystery" quality of the nature of the Scorpio female is what gives her her unpredictable magnetism. Men seem to flock around her "like moths around a flame." What's more, femme fatale that she is, she enjoys every minute of the admiration and flattery that she gets from her many adoring fans. Her appearance, regardless of her features, has the appeal of the strange loveliness of the enigmatic women of the Far East. She seems veritably made for love, if her pursuer could but break through the mystic and silent aura that is around her. To add to her allure, she uses her sense of what to wear, and will often be found out-of-style but magnificently different in some dramatic outfit.

The intense nature of this woman begins to develop early in life. She may not have many of her peers as friends, but most likely has one girl friend who shares her confidences. Towards such a pal she may have feelings of love or what she thinks is love. Another phase of her teen years is having an intense crush on a female teacher. This object of her adoration or idolatry may be the athletic type of gym instructor or her opposite, the most feminine, but sexiest, of the women teachers in her school. This may not be an exclusively Scorpio female trait except that its intensity exceeds that of girls of other Signs who share this fairly normal phase of growing up. The intensity of her emotions may take the form of suffering very profoundly. It is in this that the real Scorpio nature shows itself, for this suffering is a really deep-seated masochistic sexual pleasure. No act of perversion need be performed, yet the whole set-up is as queer as it can be.

One of the most impressive traits of the Scorpio female is her secretiveness. She knows well how to live to herself (as the New Englanders say), for herself, and by herself. She soon drops the habit of confiding in anyone, for she learns as she matures that it is easy for her to become depressed by both material trivia and delicate human relationships. A corollary to this lesson is that depression spreads easily and swiftly. Rather than be avoided by those who cannot take, and certainly not share her depressed

131

moods, she learns to rely on herself and her own company.

A major reason the Scorpio female learns self-reliance is that she is the least forgiving of the women of the entire zodiac. She is a grudge-bearer and an eternal injustice collector. Her sensitivity makes her vulnerable to the slightest hurt, real or imagined. Once a friend or lover or co-worker has trod on her emotional toes, woe unto him. She turns all Scorpion, stings to kill, and never forgets or forgives. She can alienate her whole world through her irrational reactions. Thereafter you may see her walking her dog, talking to strangers, picking up one-night stands, thinking her independence is worth her loneliness.

There is a strange contradiction in the nature of the Scorpio female in that she loves home and also loves strange places. As Scorpio is a Water Sign, many of the women born under it find employment at sea or connected with travel. They are cruise directors, nurses, or stewardesses on ocean-going ships, and love the life of going from one unusual port to another. They are not averse to having, like the sailors in an olding saying, a sweetheart in every port. Yet there is a strong tie to home. She likes one spot, be it only a small one-room apartment, to be the place that she calls home. Perhaps she is there only a few days in a whole year, but it is where she stores those things she is fond of, and where she feels she always can go. In later years, her wanderlust satisfied, she can settle down to being a fine housekeeper with a selective list of "gentlemen callers."

None of these traits of the Scorpio female bar her from getting married. Her innate radiance and charm bring many proposals. If the man she chooses is lusty, sexy, full-blooded, and able to quench the fires of her passionate nature, she can be a good wife, a real helpmate, an imaginative cook, a chic dresser, a clever home decorator, and an intellectual adviser in business matters. She is also qualified to keep her man enchained in a glorious slavery of sexual variations, going slowly, stretching out the sensuous joy, teasing, delaying, building up until the actual orgasm becomes an explosive release from pent-up sexual cliff-hanging.

In the garden of Scorpio there are many flowers. In the zoo of Scorpio there are many varieties of the Scorpion. The females of this Sign are not all alike because of the whimsical and mystic nature of the influence of Pluto on the Sign. The outstanding trait of all these is sex appeal. All, too, have consuming innate curiosity about the human body. Few are ever prudes, and most will find some sexual function for every part of their partner's bodies. The suppleness of her own physique will enable the curious Scorpio female to assume any position in the sexual act, and such positions are more likely to be aimed at exciting her partner to dizzying sexual and emotional heights than at satisfaction of her own cravings. Hers can wait until she has driven her partner half-crazy, for it is the incitement and its consequent arousal of the knowledge of her own powers that evoke the thrill in the Scorpio female.

When she has attained a kind of mental madness and a physical frenzy, then the Scorpio female takes ascendancy. Now, with her partner in the grip of her symbolic stinger, she reaches heights of sensuous delirium. She can experience a whole series of climaxes, unbelievable in number to anyone who has not actually been to bed with one of these Cleopatra's of the orgasm. At such times, anything goes, any number can play the game, and either sex or a combination of both can join in it.

133

An important factor in the life of the Scorpio female is her ambition. It is a trait that becomes interwoven in her sex life and a strong influence on the way she conducts her whole career and existence. For one thing, convention means nothing to her. For another, she will never accept a male as anything more than her own equal on any plane of being.

The triumph of the Scorpio female is well illustrated in the life and career of Mary Ann Evans, better known to the world as George Eliot. Born in obscurity, she broke every moral and social precept of her times to become one of the great figures in nineteenth century English literature. She assumed a man's name. She lived "in sin" with a man without benefit of clergy. She was an intellectual and a creative artist in an age when woman's place was in the home, protected, ignorant, compliant, and the property of her husband. Yet she lived to become a leading writer and reformer in her own time, a prophet in her own land, and the hostess to royalty on home grounds, entertaining Victoria herself, the reigning Queen and preceptor of England's most rigid morality.

What greater triumph? What does it leave to be said of the great potential of the Scorpio female except that every man should know one.

Sagittarius: November 23 to December 21

THE SAGITTARIUS MALE

November 23rd to December 21st

The Sagittarian male makes a striking appearance. He is an imposing and dramatic figure in any surroundings, and most eyes will be on him whether he is active or passive in the situation. This is a man who is deceptive but not deceiving, for while he seems to be quiescent or totally at ease or at rest, his alert mind is taking in everything around. In his secret mind, he is magnetizing some individual to turn his or her gaze upon him because he has already chosen a partner to share his bed for the night and for the future. Nor should anyone think he lacks the power to hypnotize his prey. He has depths of attraction not frequently visible nor generally ascribed to his Sign. What used to be called "animal magnetism" is not to be taken as a synonym for sex-appeal; it is a far subtler quality.

An outstanding trait of the Sagittarius male which dominates his personality is his self-confidence which is all pervading. It is attributable to success. Success leads to having money. In the case of the Sagittarius male, money leads to the development of another helpful trait, generosity.

This should not lead one to believe that the Sagittarius male's sexual conquests are buying sex in a disguised form. It is merely a fact of nature that people warm up more easily to generous folks than to penurious ones. Thus, step two in the pursuit is like an enabling clause in a contract.

With some kind of mystic foreknowledge of his future sexual conquests, the Sagittarian begins early in life to enjoy sex by himself. This may become so obsessive a practice that he continues it in adult life, seeking only to give pleasure to others while attaining his own through masturbation. This is particularly true of the Sagittarian homosexual. He seeks out very masculine active partners or rough trade, on whom he practices *fellatio* or other perversions which bring an orgasm while he is the passive party.

The self-abuse of the youth is no distinguishing trait of the Sagittarian male as it is accepted as one of nature's phases in the process of growth or maturing. Its distinction among Sagittarian males is the potential of its becoming a lifetime addiction. It may also lead to a form of love of self that alienates the individual from society, from affectionate relationships, from homo- or hetero-sexual love relationships and marriage. The typically attractive Sagittarian male needs a great deal of intuition plus experience to realize he has two pitfalls to eliminate before achieving some kind of satisfaction and self-understanding and settling into a mature pattern of life of too much admiration and the danger of falling in love with himself. The former creates complex situations in his external world; the latter, in his internal world. The "persuasion" to the passive role is not too difficult to recognize, even without feminine secondary characteristics. Females with any sophistication are turned off by the exclusively homosexual Sagittarian, who is also very likely a misogynist.

138

Should these facts present any morbid picture of the Sagittarian male, bear in mind that this is but one facet of his nature. In truth, there is nothing morbid in his nature, for he is symbolized by the Archer, a true sportsman and a real sport. This is the fellow who happily takes a chance, bets on long odds, lends money, buys the best, entertains lavishly, dresses magnificently, and lives luxuriously. He has an acquisitive nature and in the best sense of the word, for what he acquires is of value. He can acquire information, knowledge and skills which assure him a splended income, even if his life, youth or heritage have not provided him with any or a prolonged formal education. Eventually, he will acquire a cultural background by being an attentive listener (to both people and music) even if he rarely reads or retains the contents of a good book. Finally, he will acquire much of the world's goods; and his taste runs to gold and to prominence in his vocation.

There is no doubt one can have a lot of fun with the Sagittarius male. With one exception, when a serious crisis arises in his life, he will go to pieces faster than a male of any other Sign. The manliest male of his own Sign group will become as hysterical as a woman. This manly guy will immediately manifest his latent femininity by importuning all the gods, seeresses and witches to get him out of his dilemma. The same manifestation takes place when he has his heart set on some love idol and does not get it. He doesn't kneel to propose, he kneels down to implore—and sometimes to play some variation of a sexual theme.

The planet Jupiter rules the Sign Sagittarius, and the sportsmanship of the male son of the Sign leads him to places where one aspect of it occurs—gambling. This is a great temptation to the Sagittarian male. He has connections, not necessarily close ones, with the underworld, and may well be on amicable or familiar terms with touts, pimps, and panderers. His business may well be more involved with sex than with gambling, for of the two pastimes, he prefers the former. Nor does this big (or little) shot dicker about the price. He is perfectly willing to pay the going price for his fun. This kind of activity is one he really should avoid because Jupiter may bring him luck and eventually get him out of a scrape, but even Jupiter does not prevent it. It is his one vital karmic lesson, and one he learns at great expense. He must avoid open illegality in his gambling and all jail-bait in his sexual affairs.

On the negative side of the otherwise charming and enchanting Sagittarius male is a powerful tendency towards exaggeration and mendacity. To make his point or his sexual prey, he will say anything. He will swear that his glass ring is a priceless diamond, or that today is Sunday even if it is Friday. One can trust him with a loan of any amount of money, but not with the truth of any statement that he makes when he thinks it is to his advantage to misrepresent.

The racetrack tout or bookmaker type portrayed in plays, movies and books is the Sagittarian male type, especially since the symbol of the Sign is part horse. He was described as so flashily dressed as to be a caricature of the way-out style of the 20's in America and a feature of racetracks in England. Since what was way-out then is old-fashioned now, one may expect anything in the way of self-adornment from the Sagittarius male today, especially the homosexual member. These are the clients of the purveyors of the most exaggerated men's clothing shops, the caterers to embellishments in the lines of men's cosmetics, hair-dye parlors, massages, Turkish baths (including notorious ones), and jewelers who deal in the biggest of everything: links, chains, rings, tie-tacs, bands, watches, but big, shiny, and real if he can afford them. All these are tools of preening, for he must draw attention with the outer manifestation of wealth if not with wit.

Marriage is a real problem for the Sagittarius male. His problems and pitfalls have been delineated, and if he overcomes them, he marries rather late in life. Some habits have become so ingrained that real sharing of a life has become almost impossible. Besides, he does not want to give up the habits that have become his way of life, so life for his mate can be difficult. She will require superhuman tolerance and patience, be willing to overlook outburst and tantrums, and be denied many of the practices he permits himself. The latter manifestations are rationalized by the Sagittarian husband, and he tries desperately in moments of conscience-stricken contrition to make up by an expensive gift, an outpriced evening on the town, and gloriously hyperbolic expressions of love and devotion.

The zodiacal symbol of the Sign Sagittarius should be carefully studied. It is revealing. It is half horse, and the half-man is a hunter with his arrow eternally aimed at its prey.

THE SAGITTARIUS FEMALE

November 23rd to December 21st

The Sagittarius female has a feminine and delicate appearance, looking just enough out-of-this-world to appeal sexually to most men. She seems to arouse the protective instinct in the male although she may be very deceptive and misleading in this respect, though not intentionally so. Deceptive because she is really not seeking protection, for she has too much pride and self-love to feel the need. Her self-love is not exhibited in the excessive masturbation frequent with the Sagittarian boy who is the prime example of "the hand-reared boy." But she loves herself as only an exhibitionist does, desiring to adorn herself in the most luxurious wrappings, live at the best address in the finest apartment, and be seen at the smartest places. Her talk is girl talk which she prefers to intellectual conversations with men. And if the talks leads to a little fooling around in bed, she is not averse to it.

Jupiter, "the Greater Fortune," astrological Ruler of Sagittarius, is also known, less familiarly, as the eleventh-hour friend. This rulership makes the Sagittarius female lucky, as it does the male of the Sign. But the female, with her sharper intuition, tends to rely more on this aspect of Jupiter's influence. She marries late in life, not because she has had no earlier opportunities, but because she tends to dilly-dally, and she is self-satisfied. Then the right male comes along just as her family and friends have given up all hope of her ever walking to the altar. At the last moment when she has been judged a confirmed old-maid, she becomes a bride and wife. This is a fairly overwhelming experience. The loss of independence she finds regrettable. The newness, the novelty, and the glitter of marriage can reverse her whole philosophy and way of thinking and acting. The perfect wife may emerge, at least at the beginning.

The Sagittarian female is a bundle of faggots, tinder ready to be lighted, easily set on fire. With her, sex is not all-consuming as it is with other Signs, but she is ever-ready to be consumed, and it takes but a partner's pale flame to start the blaze within her. She loves her independence so much that she has little of the passion that drives other women to pursue sexual mates. Yet she loves sex, when it comes her way, and much of her life is spent making up her mind which activity will be allowed to take precedence, her willful solitary wandering or her abnegation to the one who wants her.

She is great at cruising around, finding the right spots where her type of man can be discovered and made. Yet there is a conservative and conventional streak in her makeup that holds her back from totally unconventional conduct. Despite her innate independence, it is difficult for her to throw off the fear of consequences which might be expensive socially or financially. She is also subject to the still small voice of a blessedly high degree of psychic power which emits bleeps of warning signs. Conscious of the latter, she actually feels safer in the type of hideaway mentioned, for she can assume any identity she chooses, or be anonymous, or just clown around and vanish if her intuition tells her there is some danger in what is evolving in the situation.

It is not unique for Saggittarius, both male and female, to stay pretty much near home base. Families seem to encroach upon them, make demands, need support (moral and financial) and grip them in a vise of conscience. Yet the mature Sagittarian female eventually learns the freedom and joy that new, romantic, strange and foreign scenes can give her. It is away from that home and home-bound atmosphere that she really blooms. Feeling safe from possible prying eyes of friend or relatives, she will really become a great swinger. Suddenly she is capable of picking up men (or women) and letting go—a Roman candle, lighting up the sky.

The early days of the Sagittarius female do not reveal very much of the woman into which she will evolve. Her childhood and teen-age years are governed by family rules and a sympathy and belief in conventional conduct. She takes part in sports, wears girly clothes, is a fair student, is not much of a joiner. But even in the fairly usual way with girls her age, she has special friends, or even a girl friend on which she has a crush. This might be stretched to being "mad about" some woman teacher, especially if it's a kind of masculine gym instructor. Active lesbianism is a potential, sometimes practiced, often just potential.

Marriage in the late years can be placid enough, but her mate must be physically and mentally domineering to provide any degree of happiness or even satisfaction. She keeps it cool, even as a mother, having a kind of animal attitude towards kids, a more or less "let them fend for themselves" way of regarding or ignoring them.

One must beware of the Sagittarian female, as she can be very cagey. In the social intercourse which is intended to wind up in sexual intercourse, she is well qualified to give the impression of being almost saccharine in nature, just a little innocent but very interested female—interested in the male or female who is on the make for her. But, one false remark or one drink too many, (and she needs little to get drunk and cares less about getting so) and that male or female is in for a remarkably surprising geyser of abuse. She will work herself up from seeming weakness or defenselessness into a melodramatic rage. It is then that hidden wells of strength are suddenly revealed. And it is not going to be amusing for anyone who happens to be around. There is much concealed conflict in her nature which she suffers with alone. As a result colds, chest pains, and nervous disorders are not uncommon. All are manifestations of repressed emotional conflicts. While she does not know it, this trait in her nature can easily be quieted by any student of astrology. For in truth, anyone with the nerve, courage, or daring who verbally slaps her down will emerge the instant winner. Opponents, or friends suddenly turned upon who know and remember this, will take no nonsense from the Sagittarius female. She'll give in on the first challenge. If her intended victim remains aloof, she will probably get down on her knees and beg forgiveness, or offer to do anything else that that position makes convenient.

Another tricky and deceptive trait in the Sagittarius female with her deep perception into human nature is her fall-guy reaction to wrong doers. It has some emotional connection to the gambling instinct of all Sagittarians. She will recognize a wrong male for what he is, be he gangster, mafioso, or crook. But when her heart takes the place of her head, she can convince herself that this character loves and wants her so much that he'll never take her over. The honeymoon (legal or illegal) will be absolutely ecstatic. Then the loans begin, or the need for a car, or a great business opportunity, a chance to triple *her* money. Then the till is empty, as is her bed. Beatings may commence, and then she will give him anything she has left just to get rid of him. She will recover, and if not bruised badly enough, she will fall in love with another wrongo—one who has something bigger to offer, anything, but bigger.

It is difficult for the Sagittarian female to complete any task, rarely on time if at all. This is true of her sexual, love, or romantic relationships. She is tardy at maturing, absent when required. She finds the most nebulous excuses for her vagueness, all of which she takes very seriously and believes in profoundly. She assumes a little too much to grow into a probing thinker, and can rarely part with the inner chambers of her heart's true love. They are too difficult for her to find.

Capricorn: December 22 to January 19

THE CAPRICORN MALE

December 22nd to January 19th

Unique in the family of zodiacal Signs is Capricorn. The male of the Sign may be the most difficult to fathom. He is much like the symbol of his Sign, the Sea-Goat, although the familiar and more common reference to him is simply as the Goat. In fact, there is greater revelation in the Sea-Goat symbol, for this male has the fishy quality of being submerged by reality as well as the lofty quality of the mountain-climbing goat. The discrepancies in his character and behavior are indeed difficult to understand, more difficult to justify.

Traditionally, the Capricorn male has been portrayed as cold and calculating. He is described, using the Goat symbol, as interested only in reaching heights of attainment and as being heartless as to whom he steps on on the way up. But this is far from the truth. Under a superior façade, he is one of the warmest-hearted romantics in the world. While slaying with a glance, wounding with a word, stultifying by ignoring someone, he may be burning with desire in his secret heart. For he has a heart, a great big red bleeding heart.

Why the clash between the inner and the outer Capricorn male? It is to be attributed to the rulership of his Sign by the planet Saturn. This heavenly orb gave rise to the descriptive adjective, saturnine—dour, dark, foreboding. He feels that joy has a price. Saturn, as the celestial school master, insists that one do his homework or he will be punished. This is all a part of an innately clever mind's work. While he is at a party, his mind and conscience will be telling him how he could better or more profitably spend his time. But his body is telling him to try a conquest, to get the best looking female at the party into his apartment and into his bed. And soon thereafter into his heart because he is a real lover under that ambitious front, and a real sucker for the one who knows how to make him feel loved.

Capricorn is an Earth Sign, and it cannot be taken away from the Capricorn male that he is an earthy being. He is right down in the dirt, has no inhibitions, will listen to anything, and enjoy wallowing. Once again, this is a hidden trait, but hidden only from those he does not trust. The latter will know him as a most dignified, moral, conventional man. His cronies will know him as a blockbuster with the strength and moral fiber of a tank and a vocabulary that would put the heavy pornography writers to shame. His repertoire of anecdotes and stories is so vast that he has one to expatiate on every situation. It takes a lot to warm him up, but once he is running, the rest of the crowd had better sit up and pay attention.

The earthy Capricorn male discovers his genitalia at a very early age. His wonder and imagination are stirred, and so is his curiosity. Then no end of pleasure seems to be his. He eventually engages in sexual play with other young boys.

In due course he learns that girls are physically

different, and they become an object of his interest and desire. No one ever played doctor with as deep a seriousness as the Capricorn male. Tag, post-office, sports, are soon abandoned. This lad wants to play doctor, and with as many patients as his schedule permits.

A serious problem in the sex drive of the Capricorn male is the strong tendency to homosexual attachments. It is interesting to note that this is one of the precepts of Hindu astrology also. This is a serious problem, even if the Capricorn male never so much as touches another man, because the latent desire is there. It is an innate characteristic. He may experiment, he may be the passive party to the act, he may become a flagrant deviate. But these are not characteristic, for Saturn, Ruler of his Sign, is always there, like the Freudian unconscious censor, saying, "remember the price you will have to pay if you do what you would like to do." The stifling effects of repression lead to other outlets, just as total sexual repression can be converted into Freudian sublimation. The same energy can make him a Don Juan, a heroic womanizer, or a public figure who leads in great reform movements. Still, he may also sneak looks at another male in the urinal at his club.

Whether his prey be male or female, the mature Capricorn man is a lover anyone would find desirous to please, fulfilling, and terribly tender although he does not restrain his potent love-making in any way. *The Love Machine* is not a television set, no matter what the author of that book says; it is a healthy, sensual Capricorn male.

Profound understanding of human nature and an innate sense of how to arouse a woman or a man make him desirable, sought after, and almost never happy. He is kind, generous, and thoughtful. He buys gifts for his bedmates,

151

sends novel and original letters or poems to them, and feels nothing he does is rewarding enough for all the effort he puts forth. He has internal and intestinal combustion from thwarted romantic notions that date back into a seeming infinity of past incarnations. The Man of Sorrows was born while the Sun was in Capricorn.

When the Capricorn man emerges from the Capricorn youth, he is fully experienced, has certain ideals, and definitely retains the image of perfect true love in the romantic sense. He is ready for marriage, but picky and choosy. Poetic love stories have filled his mind, and he wants to be half of one of the great love affairs of history—Paolo to Francesca, Romeo to Juliet, Pinkerton to Butterfly, maybe Oscar Wilde to Lord Alfred Douglas or Lord Alfred to Oscar. As he becomes an even greater lover with maturity, he maintains his appeal and even finds that it is enhanced as he grows older, for Capricornians are the happiest geriatrics in the world. Their luck increases as they grow older. Marriage is more common after thirty than before. The Capricorn husband is a' great stud in bed. He may be jealous, demanding, vengeful, out of bed. These are the outbursts of his frustrations when he imagines he is rejected or unloved, for beneath his orderly and conventional exterior is the callow youth who wants to be told every minute that his lover loves him.

This portrait must not detract from the outer man's impressive personality. He dresses well, speaks eloquently, and can be a real merrymaker. Long lived, he appears to improve in looks as time goes on. This is a great help to his changing fancies, for whereas he likes them older when he is young, he likes them younger when he is old.

The wandering eye of this perpetual lover may light

upon a partner from any socio-economic-ethnic group, and catch an answering affirmation. Snob that he is in society, he enjoys enormously sexual experiences with a common lout or anonymous female in a roadside motel and is capable of carrying on such an alliance through the years, whether he is married or single.

It is no easy matter to love the Capricorn male. He is jealous, vengeful, and clever. But allied to the right mate, he is the best, sweetest, kindest cheat in the whole world.

THE CAPRICORN FEMALE

December 22nd to January 19th

The Capricorn female sex life is more in conformity with the symbol of the Sign than is the Capricorn male's sex life. The Sea-Goat is capable of leading a double life as it has the body of a land animal and the tail of a fish. The Capricorn female is qualified to enjoy sex with males and females. The word "enjoy" is used because every female is qualified to partake of intercourse with both sexes, but it is the Capricorn Lady who is both *qualified* and *enjoys* it.

This qualification or tendency is not intended to stigmatize the Capricorn female as an innate lesbian. She is rarely an aggressive masculine-like pursuer of other women. On the other hand, her likes make her bisexual. She prefers to be passive, letting the lesbian do the pursuing and indulging in her personal form of sexual perversion. The Capricorn female enjoys the peripheral activities such as, the idea of having a "best friend" or "my closest friend." She likes the emotional content of the relationship, receiving flowers and gifts, sneaking off to secret lunches, telephoning

154

her girl friend from a party to which she has gone with a man, perhaps her fiancé or husband.

She also likes to get a bit drunk with her butch lover, but rarely "goes all the way" herself in the sex act unless she has been well-oiled by her favorite drinks which lets her guard down. She can evade, excuse or rationalize her instinctive guilt the next day by blaming her conduct on having been drunk or else going through a convenient alcoholic amnesia.

The Capricorn female is a tower of strengths. She has physical endurance except for an inclination towards forms of arthritis and rheumatism. Her strength is also spiritual and will-powered. The lady is a commander of women, men, attention, respect, adulation and numerous weaklings who attach themselves to her as self-adopted children, lovers, learners, pleaders, and emotional beggars.

The Capricorn female who is typical of her Sign gives the impression of being a born aristocrat, as indeed she is. Capricorn is at the zenith of the natural zodiac. It has always been there, even through changes in the calendar made by man in his perverting (not converting) the clock in the sky which never needs winding. The technical explanation of this unique phenomenon is accurately delineated in the 1971 *American Astrology Digest.*

A haughty bearing and an overbearing haughtiness are actually sexual characteristics of the Capricorn female as well as the Capricorn male. She is a slave driver in her bedroom, and the use of the whip need not be thought disgusting to her. In appearance, however, no such trait is in evidence, for she has an autocratic and lithe gait, and gives the impression of being tall and thin even if she is not. She has the hottest come-hither look which she can turn into one of freezing disdain at a moment's notice. Whatever her mood, she is impressive, sexually attractive, masterful, tantalizing, and able to retain her appeal until a ripe old age. To the Capricorn female, it is one of life's charms that she retains her youthful looks and sexual attraction. Her golden years may bring even greater sexual satisfaction than those of her salad days. It was to Cleopatra that this reference was made, for her judgment "then was green." This may well be applied to the Capricorn female. In youth she is less discriminating in her choice of sex partners. In maturity her judgment becomes far more eclectic. Also, like Cleopatra, she retains her magnetism for men and women of authority, influence, and power far past the age when women of other Signs are resigned to motherhood or spinsterhood or keeping a cat for company. Truly, the Capricorn woman has more to be grateful for than she ever admits. She sometimes even resents her own glorious gifts.

It takes a crisis or a catastrophe to understand the Capricorn female fully. She is at her best when all hell breaks loose. She is jealous beyond women of any other Sign, and this trait is sufficient to make her have a very low boiling point. Discovery of any act of disloyalty, cheating, going behind her back, gossiping, hurting her reputation, being niggardly, chicanery, penury or adultery will bring on a scene almost unbelievable in its violence—certainly unpredictable in a woman with such a calm and controlled exterior.

Yet, when her beloved is in trouble, sick, in financial need, delinquent in some duty, falsely accused, unjustly fired, she is a bastion of protectiveness, a tigress against the enemy, a balm to melancholy. As a restorer of self-confidence, as a comforter, as a solace, as a complete symbol of motherhood, she is all-embracing, all-smothering, all love!

Lucky is the individual in trouble who has a Capricorn lady lover!

Early in life the Capricorn female gives in to her intense curiosity about sex. She is remarkable in her innocence, for she fails to know right from wrong, so young is she when the stirrings of sex arouse her. This girl asks questions that may embarrass or amuse her parents, depending on their own socio-economic background. She will "discover" words and pictures in the dictionary that arouse sexual fantasies, and the pets and relatives she can have contact with help to do little to assuage her early heats and ignorant frustrations.

Experimentation becomes a very time-consuming activity, and she is game for anything, but inclined to be very secretive. She is fairly successful at naive conquests and gets them to swear to secrecy. At this stage, she is a hoarder, in the sense that she will keep a diary, count up how many experiences she has had before she falls asleep, and look forward to enlarging the number of whatever she is after. Numbers mean a lot, and she intends to have them.

One of the emotional problems of the Capricorn female is discovering a mate—butch or stud—who is always as highly keyed and ready for sex as she is. Despite the superior attitude and impression she makes because of the traits endowed upon her by her Sign's being at the top of the zodiac, she is really a hot-blooded creature. That stand-away air she exhibits on first meeting is a protective psychological device. It is an armor. Under it all, she is avid for sexual experiences.

She is a hidden volcano, and when she erupts, her lover knows she has been loved, and so does she. She is ready and available all the time. Where does she find a partner who can perform as she can? This is the problem we began with. One of the answers is indeed unique. She finds, if she is willing, quite a number, not too intelligent, not too rich, maybe even poor, are available. He knows or they know what to do and she can surreptitiously carry on with a type like this for years. Such a concealed and secret affair can make for great sexual and emotional satisfaction because of its secrecy and because she can really let go all her inhibitions and act out all her fantasies.

The Capricorn female has great virtues in addition to the complexity of the combination of all her other traits. She makes a wonderful silent partner in affairs, other than sexual, of those, or the one, she loves. The subtle way she has of injecting ambition and inspiration are a wonder to behold. Her patience with a loved one is infinite, especially in comparison with her disdain for the stupidity of ordinary mortals. She seeks to raise her lover to her own position: the top of the zodiac, where her birth has placed her and where she deserves to be.

Aquarius: January 20 to February 18

THE AQUARIUS MALE

January 20th to February 18th

Probably the most famous Aquarius male in the history of the world was Franklin D. Roosevelt. This is not an analysis of his personal life, but he is given as an example of the complexity of the nature, makeup and character of the type of man born under the Sign of Aquarius. One can understand some of this complexity if he appreciates the vast, almost infinite, changes that have taken place in recent years. If one ponders and muses on what "This is the Age of Aquarius" means, on the revolution that has taken place in dress, manners, morality, religion, warfare, and living, one gets some idea of the power in the word Aquarius.

If a slogan were to be chosen to be put upon a banner declaring the sexual attitude, outlook, and philosophy of the Aquarian, there is an old Latin one that fits to perfection: *Et quid amabo nisi est Quod aenigma est?* "What shall I love unless it be the enigma?"

The Aquarian is a lover of mystery. In this matter we respectfully cite the late F.D.R.'s love of mystery stories. He had Alexander Woollcott at the White House frequently during World War II as a connoisseur to choose books to go to bed with. Sexually, the Aquarius male is a constant experimenter in sex—not a "constant reader." To probe into the enigma of the personality and sex life of everyone is his aim. His innate curiosity knows no bounds, and he is like a brilliant district attorney or prosecutor in his questioning, his searching queries, his psychic ability to get to the root of the matter. In this respect, he may be called a radical, for the origin of this word is root—getting to the root *is* radical. His profound interest in everybody's sex life is catholic, that is to say, universal. One may be amazed at the scope and startling power of his interests and interrogations, and then may discover himself as the object of his curiosity or of his sexual attack.

The Aquarius male does not necessarily appear to have much sexual drive. He looks frequently like the most conventional type or even more like a weakling than a stud. The appearance is deceiving, for beneath it lies a male with potency sufficient to take care of a good-sized harem. It is an asset to his making conquests that he seems to be so neutral or non-aggressive, for the object of his desires is put off guard by his apparent affability.

So selfless does he seem that it takes a rare psychic perception to pierce the armor of his outward personality. The Piscean type might see through this more readily than members of the other Sign groups. But let it be clearly understood that the Aquarius male innately produces more protein, calcium, and testosterone within his body than the surface can show, and naturally this leads to potency and virility which make him the Casanova of his world. Like Casanova, too, he regrets the waning of his sex energy no matter what age this inevitable change begins to take place.

The symbol of the Sign is the Water-Bearer, depicted as a male pouring water out of a vessel. The spiritual interpretation of this is that he is pouring out the water of the soul. This symbolizes his zodiacal role; the humanitarian. Also, occultly, he receives in return favors from fortune, dowries from destiny, and fame from philanthropy. Physically interpreted, the symbol indicates that his sexual prowess gives pleasure which is returned by his wife, mistresses, lovers, and strangers in the night.

The Aquarius male is also the receiver of admiration, which is duly deserved on all levels, physical, sexual, spiritual, moral, and social. The negative aspect of this part of his life is that he is also the receiver of flattery, and his innate goodness can make him a victim of this fine trait. This also applies to his sex life. His sincere admirers, his flatterers, and the purely selfish who fawn upon him soon learn that this is an original guy who cannot say no. So the onslaught takes place, and he becomes the victim of those who really only want to use him to satisfy their own cravings and desires. Fortunately, he is well enough endowed to fulfill the demands made upon him.

In youth, the Aquarius male has more of a sense of conscience than members of other Signs. He is obedient and dutiful, and a joy to his parents and relatives as he evinces the sense of responsibility which is an inborn attribute. The attention he pays to the young girls and little old ladies in his social group seems most admirable to his teachers and other elders. But it is the same trait which he later uses in his pursuit of his sexual prey. The same attentiveness and gallantry become the ammunition with which he bombards those whom he wishes to take to bed. This change is immoral if one takes the point of view of T. S. Eliot in *Murder in the Cathedral*—the good acts based on bad motives are immoral.

Marriage is the high point in the sex life of the Aquarius male. Bound in public by all the conventions regardless of his sexual propensities, this man wants a wife who will, if anything, improve his own social status. He is a club man, and would not bring into his world a woman who is less than his equal. For this reason, he is choosy about the woman whom he gives his name. He wants someone of whom to be proud, for her birth, but particularly for her cultural attainments. This may delay marriage until late in life, but success in finding such a mate will double his pleasure. It means a higher rung on the social ladder plus enhanced sexual pleasure as his excitation is increased by a woman whom his world considers so "high class" as to be almost above having sexual intercourse.

While passion plays the greatest role in his single and married life, the Aquarius male is not consumed by it. The reason is that he actually lives for the moment—the here and now. He can adjust himself to any situation, to any place. Were a plane to set him down alone in some unique community, he would feel little or no regret. He would take inventory of his situation, settle himself within it, and soon campaign for ways in which to ameliorate his own circumstances and the entire environment. This adds up to the Aquarius male's ability to find a new love after marriage, get a divorce, and start a new married life without a regret or a backward glance. He demands and gets the cooperation of his spouse or lover, in bed and out of it.

It must always be borne in mind that the Aquarius male is a law unto himself, otherwise real understanding of him will never be accomplished. Even so, understanding him is very difficult because he is so complex. The complexity of his whole personality is involved with his sex life. He is the standard bearer of morality in his home and community, but everything he does in bed is natural to him, and he can think up some curious deviations.

The man is a born analyst. No human relationship is too involved or too complex for him to tackle and to solve. In his sexual partnerships he is just as perceptive as he is at seeing through others. He is inclined to be secretive about his feelings towards the one he loves, but if body language and mental telepathy really work, his lover will know just what his feelings are without words. This character is really worthwhile because he will always give more than he gets.

THE AQUARIUS FEMALE

January 20th to February 18th

The Aquarius female may be the biggest surprise package you ever open when you try to analyze her character. In going into depth in studying her sex life, you may discover that the package is either a Pandora's box or that it contains a bomb.

The element of surprise lies in the fact that the Sign Aquarius is noted for its bestowing such idealistic traits upon its sons and daughters. They are known for their idealism, humanitarianism, and for a universal love which is their deep-seated religion, far more than is any orthodox belief.

These individuals, especially the females of the Sign, do good without being objectionable or obnoxious do-gooders. The Aquarius female is innately desirous of helping others—all others, not merely those close to her, as family or friends, but everyone. She has been characterized by astrology as being so akin to all mankind that her love for those near to her can be no greater than her love for the world. In one sense this traditional description is unfair; her love for family and friends is not diminished because she loves the world, it is, in fact, more intense. The Aquarius female wants to be the mother of her own mother and father, brothers and sisters. Rather than being impersonal about them, she tends to smother them with attention, gifts, and concern. Stressed as this trait is, she can become a burden to those she loves, although she is never conscious of it.

All this makes it unique that the Aquarius female is the most sexually liberated of women. She needs no organized group to show her the way to obtaining liberation because she was born with it. The Women's Lib movement strikes the Aquarius female as an unnecessary joke on her own sex. Unmarried and pregnant, she must have the biggest laugh in the world watching the gals go by bearing banners with their demands. It is difficult to realize the two Aquarius females who have borne illegitimate children, Mia Farrow and Vanessa Redgrave, demanding their rights or joining Women's Lib. They were, and are bearing children and letting the whole world know about it. They did not consider their unmarried status nor the marital status of the men who are the fathers of their children.

Heat is not the basis of the Aquarius female's conduct, such as that of the two stars mentioned. She is not solely motivated by the desire to mate or rut. Rather does she mate because of the ideal love that she has found. Dryden titled his play about Cleopatra "All For Love, or the World well Lost." There is an affinity with this title and the slogan of the Aquarius female—with an exception. It is that her slogan is truly "All For Love," *but* there will be no world lost. This woman will have love and hold the world in her palm as her personal possession. She has been far ahead of her times throughout the ages.

Courageous enough to have fought for her rights in

the past, to have been an idealistic reformer but not a blue-nose, the Aquarius female's motives are pure. In the same way, so is her love because the drive towards sexuality is greatly sublimated towards love, romance, friendship with her mate, and a helpfulness beyond compare. These latter traits frequently are the cause of friction and misunderstanding, as men interpret all this warmth as an urge to get them into bed. What the Aquarius female's conduct really means is, "Let's get together and help somebody." *Not* "Let's get together and make love."

The Aquarius female's aim in sex is to experience it in the tender ways remotely described in Victorian novels. She likes to be courted with poetry, in romantic settings, in gentle and veiled terms, and never with gross vulgarities, haste, or any circumstances or situation that might be described as sordid. Never repelled by sex itself, the physical mating without the aura of love and glamor of romance leaves the Aquarius female cold.

To generate heat for a valid and enjoyable sexual experience, the sex partner of the Aquarius female must understand her basic reactions. She is not generally put into the mood by petting, necking, touching, or any of the possible erotic perversions which so often precede coitus. Rather will she respond to poetic and romantic whisperings of love and a gentle show of affection, with desire as the symbol of the expression of love rather than as a separated activity. For these reasons, she builds up slowly in the sexual union. While the partner is seeking satisfaction, or possibly the greatest thrills in variety and number, the Aquarius female is in a languorous dream mood, taking all the passion being generated as body language of love. Thus she will have her orgasm once, then linger in the arms of love, which may hold more significance and pleasure for her than the orgasm heights she has just experienced.

Besides her charm and friendliness, the Aquarius female has natural charms in her physical makeup. They are rarely over normal height and tend to be shorter and smaller than the distaff side of other Signs. The hair and complexion are frequently shades of brown or true black, infrequently, natural blonde although the eyes can make for unusual combinations such as blue or violet with black hair. It is the expression of the eyes which distinguishes the Aquarian, for it reflects her innate idealism and therefore gives (a correct) impression of dreaminess, of being far away in spirit, or seeing objects, people, or events that are happening on the astral plane but not yet upon the earth. The stare or the penetrating look one gets when she is concentrating on someone is accompanied by a downward glance or turning her head to one side. It is provocative indeed, but it also invariably succeeds in getting the answer or the information she is after. She should never be lassoed—never can be—because her mind is on that distant place only she can see, and which she will never share, certainly not with anyone she is sexually intimate with.

The details of the picture so far drawn of the Aquarius female seem to fail to make her qualified for marriage in the ordinary or normal way. This should be enough to put off any man who wants torrid sex every night in the week and sometimes at lunch or a matinee. Individual Aquarius females, but not the typical ones, may be very sensual. These are the exceptions whose Moon and Venus are in sensitive zones of their personal horoscopes. The traits of the Aquarius female do not, however, bar her from being an excellent wife in all other respects. She is not one to nag or interfere with her husband's interests. She is not one to suspect him of other liaisons, and is herself above suspicion. The reason is not her overpowering need for her mate, but the variety of her own interests and the respect she has for him and his. She has all the social graces, makes a refined appearance, and is an adornment to her home, husband and social group.

The symbol of the Sign Aquarius is the Water-Bearer. The influence of this symbolism is the same for the Aquarius female as for the Aquarius male. It is representative of the Aquarian's pouring out the waters of the soul, the cleansing of the individual and the world, the spiritual illumination of mankind. This alone would preclude any clandestine relationship. It explains the two movie stars openly having their children—an event for all to see, regardless of the world's opinion.

The Sign's planetary ruler is Uranus. The reign of this heavenly body is lightning-like and electrical. It heralded and was responsible for electricity and the changes it has wrought. The ladies born under its rulership are the heralds of the future. The coming trends in sexuality and its changing customs and mores are all here for you to see; just keep your eye on the Aquarius female.

Pisces: February 19 to March 20

February 19th to March 20th

Astrology is a branch of occultism, the study of the mysteries behind the veil. Pisces is the astrological ruler of occultism and the people born while the Sun transits this Sign are sensitives, psychics, mediums; they are perceptive, prophetic, intuitive. All these traits are interwoven with their sex lives, and those who fall for Pisceans will learn that they experience the greatest vicissitudes of all living humans.

In dealing with the Pisces male, one must realize that regardless of age, race, creed, or physical appearance, he is loaded with sex appeal. He may be bald and chubby Zero Mostel, or Harry Belafonte, talented Nureyev or warped Nijinsky, but he will reek of sensuality, that bedroom scent, that ineffable and overpowering exudation, sex. In addition to the potent quality and the quality of potency, the Pisces male is pathologically involved with sex. It pervades his mentality and his physical organsim. It is the basic motivating force in his highest ideals, in his greatest achievements, in his etherealized love, in all that the flesh experiences and in all that the flesh transcends.

With such an obsession, can the Pisces male lead what the world calls a normal life? Not only can he, but he has the potential of surpassing normal success in every department of life. This is so even though he may be heterosexual, homosexual, or one of sex's freaks. He is a pursuer of sexual prey, but filled with romantic dreams at the same time. He is filled with the surging impulses of poetic and chivalric love while simultaneously the rhythm of sex is beating in his heart and the blood is coursing through his veins.

The Pisces male is the most introverted one in the entire zodiacal family of the Signs. The mystic element and his inborn (even if it is unconscious) mediumship make him terribly empathetic. He may not even know why this is his condition, but it is one very difficult to cope with. The Pisces male can take on all the troubles of the people in his world. He is really like a young man studying medicine and contracting each new disease as he studies it in his imagination. In the case of the Pisces male, this condition is very real, not imaginary. He genuinely suffers—so magnetic is he to the suffering of others.

Strangely, for this reason it is more difficult for him to attract gay or happy conditions. There is a whole segment of the world wearing clown masks—the men of Pisces. The man at the party flattering some old unattractive woman, smiling at her, lighting her cigarette, having another drink himself, and saying "Marvelous party" is the Pisces male. He is playing his role, his game. And he is so good at it that he believes he is enjoying himself.

Alcohol is one of his problems. The Pisces male at the party will drink more than anyone else. After all, his dreams are not coming true; they are too, too big to be realized.

Drink makes the world seem rosier; it releases the frustrations; it puts a veil over the failures; it gives him a real hangover in the morning. And the only cure is a hair from the dog that bit him. The cycle starts again. Addiction of any kind is a problem for the Pisces male because he has a very hard time with reality. Whether it starts with the codeine in cough medicine or a shot for pain, he must completely avoid any and all kinds of mood pills, narcotics, and alcohol. Those Pisces men who are hooked, habitual drunks, or sick, soon discover their sex powers have vanished. This becomes just another excuse to the weak ones to further indulge in the bottle, the needle, or the weed. Doctors and astrologers should be on the alert to save the beautiful Pisces male for sex.

A movie star of great age who attempted to portray a young woman in a sex movie was described by one critic as "looking like something that was pasted together." This phrase could be applied to the emotional body (an occult Hindu term) of the Pisces male. He seems to be unstrung, or at loose emotional ends, when it comes to his love life. Generous to a fault, he expects as much from the one he loves. His giving has no end, materially and romantically. Should he have chosen some coarse or undeveloped lover, he will be deeply wounded, for few have the depth of understanding to realize how much the Pisces male needs to be loved in return, how sensitive he is, how big a human being he is, how kind he is, how unselfish he is. Perceiving finally that his sex partner or lover does not have the capacity to attain the emotional and spiritual heights he reaches, the Pisces male moves down into a slough of despondency. He learns he might have been better off with someone above him, or at least able to dominate him. Alas, he learns too late.

The sexual act is a subtle ritual for the Pisces male. There is always the necessity for the big build-up. This is not a matter of time, but of emotional and intellectual *timing.* The understanding might take place simultaneously between him and the chosen and accepting partner, but there will be no hasty mating. This must be preceded by the acting out of his own fantasies and some kind of schedule or program that he has worked out in his head or which becomes a habit through repetition. It may start with question and answer. It may go on with a friendly drink. It can diverge to likes and dislikes. Then comes identification. Note: *not* before! Then another drink or some small talk. And then it begins and ends in silence. But between the beginning and the ending there can occur every kind of murmur, grunt, noise, but no words. And the acts—name anything in the dictionary of perversions, and they are there. Nor is one to think this lacks tenderness, nor that there is anything that does not "come naturally." All is part of the act of love. Whether this mating is between the Pisces male and a pick-up or between him and a lover with a regular status, everything in the act is an act of love. As long as it lasts.

Because it is easy to take advantage of the Pisces male, many people do so. This brings a strange reversal of the sensitive reaction of the Pisces male. He is so sympathetic to others that when they suffer physically or emotionally or wound him, you will see a real tragedian emerge from this dual personality. He will weep, bleed, and scream in his agony of having had his feelings hurt or his trust broken. There is only one way to react to this—ignore the whole thing.

The Piscean male has so much innate knowledge of life that he makes a difficult student. He has lived through so many incarnations, is such an old soul, that he takes direction badly. Maturity in the worldly sense is difficult for him to attain. Facing reality is the same problem. Facing the realities of sexual union may also be too much of a practical problem for him.

Perhaps in the winter of his discontent the Pisces male will discover his one true love—himself.

THE PISCES FEMALE

February 19th to March 20th

The female born under the Sign Pisces develops a makeup, a totality of character, completely in keeping with the symbol of her Sign, the Two Fish. In the symbol, one fish is going upstream, one, downstream. Like Gemini, this is a Double Sign, but the Twins of Gemini are side by side. The Fish in Pisces are going in opposite directions. There is strong duality in the nature of the Pisces female. She is the noblest idealist of the females of the human race, she has also been dubbed the whore of the zodiac. Upstream she goes, struggling valiantly like the salmon against the tide, then downstream, into the effluvia of degradation, perhaps hitting the muddy bottom of disgrace and social banishment.

Were there ever a model of saintly humanitarianism, it would be the Pisces female. Were there ever one of the femme fatale, of the Circe who turned men into swine, of the vampire who destroyed her lovers, it would be the Pisces female.

How can such a split personality exist in a world

where sophistication reaches down to even the lowest socio-economic levels, where kids are as wise as their parents, when all the obscene words and all the perversions are commonplace to the unwashed and the unlettered? Easily. She can exist; she can survive; she can surpass her sisters in every competitive activity—the arts, business, home life, and in love. Her duality is accompanied by duplicity. In the art of acting out her role, no Bernhardt, no Bette Davis, no Katherine Cornell could give as realistic nor as stirring a performance.

How does she do it? The Piscean female is a mistress of illusion. Because her Sign is under the astrological rulership of Neptune, planet of imagery, of conversion, of change, of changelings. The deceptions of Nature herself are ruled by Neptune: the rainbow in the sky, the mirage in the desert. The deceptions of progress are also under Neptune's rulership: the lifelike images on the motion picture screen, the conjurer's art. Thus the Piscean female has no difficulty in creating the illusion, the picture or vision of herself, as she wants her world to see her. Developed in mediumship, she will be a great medium. Beneath her art and artifice may dwell a great courtesan, an adulteress, a lesbian, a necrophiliac. Her obsession may take her on visits to hell itself, but there will be no experience that she will deny herself.

There is little for her to deny herself because practically every man is ready and willing to give the Pisces female just about anything her heart desires. While the Pisces female tends to be dark and shining, there are those (depending on their Rising Sign) who are light complexioned with green eyes. It does not seem to matter to the men whether the Pisces female is typical of her Sign traits or not;

all the men know is that she exudes sex appeal and to have her is their fondest wish.

The best-selling book, *Feminine Mystique,* might well have been dedicated to the Pisces female, for the two words in the title are the best possible description of her distinction. She is well aware of this quality. If she were ever honestly modest, the praise she gets would soon remove this. Then, too, she has a natural desire to show off her beauty and charm—natural because it is inborn. She is the preening bird of paradise displaying all her endowments to get a male, as nature demands, for humans cannot yet reproduce without a contribution from each of the sexes.

The entire span of the sex life of the Pisces female is strongly influenced by her relationship with her father. The early years of this woman's psyche are molded and sculpted by the male parent, and the subsequent years are a reflection of it. Her sexual habits will relate to the happiness or the misery of childhood and girlhood, although there are all kinds of variations and degrees of emotional living between the extremes of love or hate that existed. This frequently results in a search for love in a father image, cliché though this description may seem to be. It brings about multiple marriages, but the best is always the masterful man, who can and wants to dominate the woman.

Stalin's daughter is alleged to have been married twice in Russia. She found and lost her great romantic love in India, and settled down in America to wifehood and motherhood. From her revelations, it appears her search was for security, obviously because of the terror she experienced with her father. One of the world's most glittering movie stars has been married many times. This Piscean beauty has had two successful marriages, one which ended in the death of her husband, the present one being one of the greatest romances of today's world. The lasting ones have been with men of tremendous strength of character, and it seems as though Liz and Dick Burton will be married a long, long time.

The man's dominance over the Pisces female is necessary because her moods are almost unpredictable. She is the most temperamental woman of any of the Signs of the zodiac. She can go from shy to brash in the wink of an eye. She can hide herself away from the world or give such a display of foul temper and language that the auditor may well tremble. She can be the most genteel lady at the Court of St. James or swear like a longshoreman if she doesn't get her way.

The storm and strife of her moods and emotional turmoil may lead to various forms of very dangerous attempts to escape from frustrations, real or imaginary. The most frequent escape the Pisces female turns to is alcohol, and this gal can really drink like the fish which is the symbol of her Sign. In some cases, she turns to mood pills, equally dangerous if this becomes habitual. Narcotics may be an outlet, begun perhaps in desperation or as an experiment, and ending by her being trapped in the living death.

Needing to be loved, wanted, and possessed, the Pisces female is equally generous in the love she gives her man and children. She is capable of fooling people, however, for she often pulls a very tough act. Qualified as a fine actress, she can play the role of the sophisticated woman of the world—a real wit, cynic, or a hard-boiled woman. All this is a cover for the essential tenderness too often hidden under that veneer of self-confidence and toughness. Observed with her brood, one can see the profound love she lavishes on the ugly duckling.

The Pisces female is sensual, with the ability to use her looks, charm, and sex appeal professionally as an actress, model, hostess, receptionist, or public relations executive. The same qualities that appeal to her men make her popular with the public. She takes deep satisfaction in the appreciation of her personality, and when the physical aspects of her charm begin to fade, she puts up a pretty good fight to restore or preserve them. This gal doesn't want to lose, and she will never throw her towel in the ring. She will use it to wipe up the cosmetics, paints, powders, and whatever artifice she can discover to hide or disguise her vanishing luminosity. She will succeed, too, for she is ruled by Neptune, the planet of illusion.

Summing her up, illusion may be the one real thing about the Pisces female. Grasp her in your arms, and you may find all you are holding is a mirage.

sexual
compatibility
guide

Since the sexual act normally involves two people, the guidance given in this section will not separate the sexes in the readings given. Each Sign heading applies to both males and females, and exposes the potential relationship between them whether it be compatible or hostile.

To derive the greatest benefit from this section, read the guide given for your own Sign; then read the guide for the Sign of the person you wish to know about—whether lover, potential lover, or possible choice of mate.

ARIES

Men and women born under Aries are all achievers. They have more up-and-go than members of almost all other Signs, perhaps even more ambition than all the other Signs put together. This same push, enthusiasm, and ardor applies to their love lives. Aries-born people have enormous drive, overpowering emotions, and tremendous physical desires. Sex is their outstanding experience, and they cannot seem to conceive of a life that consists of suppression, repression, or lack of love—to them the greatest of all human feelings.

Love between people born under Aries and another Sign may not survive the potency of the Arians' emotions. They are so volatile that the slightest tremor, change, or facial expression can put them far off intellectually, sentimentally, and even geographically. A slight, a forgotten birthday on the part of the loved one, and love may very easily fly out of the window! On to the next love; forget the old and on with the new—that is the cry of Aries no matter how much they suffer, and suffer they do, indeed.

The fact that Aries is the first Sign of the zodiac makes all those born under it natural leaders. Therefore they have every qualification for success, in every field of endeavor: in business, social life, home life, and in the bedroom. They are practical people, even where their own emotions are involved. When it comes to experiencing sex, they will never take the promise for the deed. With them it is put out or get out!

A person born under Leo would make the best sex partner and mate for the Aries group. Because sex is so great a part of their lives, Aries people will find an outlet, a balance, and a constancy in the Sun-ruled Leo family. Ardor is also typical of the Leo-born, so there would be no problem of having to bear up under the objections or repressions possible with members of other Sign groups. If the Aries person is faithful, loving, and attentive, the mate he or she has chosen from the Leo family will make for a happy and long-lived marriage or extra-marital type relationship.

Another Sign group which can help the Aries group in sex and in all life's aspects is Taurus. The slower pace at which Taurus travels will lessen the rush, the hustle and bustle of the Aries way of living. The sexual impetuosity of Aries can be toned down by Taurus, and the Aries partner could develop even greater sexual prowess through this emotional partnership.

It must be emphasized that each individual has many more influences in his or her chart than just the Sun's, which determines the Sign. Where marriage is concerned, certainly the two parties should have comparative horoscopes made up by a specialist in astrology.

The impetuous nature of Aries will be cooled by people born under the Air Signs: Gemini, Libra and Aquarius. The Water Signs would be too delicate for them. As for the Earth Signs: they should stay away from Aries—they would be bored to infinity.

TAURUS

The powerful rulership of Venus, planet of love and beauty, over people born under the Sign Taurus is the influence which makes them so filled with desire and so desirable. Mating or marriage and Taurus could by synonyms (for Taurus). These natives of the Sign are innately marriage-minded, so much so that they usually marry at a much younger age than do natives of other Signs.

Taurean folks love their homes, want a lot of children, and seek to establish beauty and harmony all around them.

Sons and daughters of the Sign Taurus have very profound sentimental and sexual feelings which they do not find easy to express despite their depth, or *because* they are not on the surface. However, though they may not be eloquent, vocal, or articulate, they have persistence. This makes their pursuit of love and sex subtle and successful, for they can win out through a lengthy and patient courtship, whereas less durable competitors, although more bombastic, will lose out.

The honesty, sincerity, and straighforwardness of Taurean people makes their love pure—for the majority. They can be taken advantage of because of these traits, but as they are very intelligent, experience soon teaches them how to guard and protect themselves against love vultures. Sexual virility is another advantage that helps them, for Taureans (Sign of the Bull) retain sexual youthfulness until old age.

Mating with a member of the Aquarius Sign group is the best choice for Taureans. There is a wonderful balance established in such a combination. The virility of the Taurus-born combined with the thoughtfulness and logic of the Aquarian makes for a lasting union.

People born under Earth Signs will form a different kind of union with Taurus people. Virgo and Capricorn will understand the material outlook that Taurus people have. The combination makes for ambition and success even if it is not crowned with great emotional ecstasy.

The more emotional Water Sign people will lean on the Taureans for strength, support, and will be partners of a union in which they take more than they give.

To the Taureans, Air Sign people other than Aquarius

are an enigma. The Taurus person will be bewildered by the dreamy character of those born under Gemini and Libra.

Sex and marriage with people born under the Fire Signs could fail because this type of combination can wear each partner out physically and emotionally. It is too intense to last very long.

In all cases, the Taurus person has a steadfastness that makes for sticking with a bargain, even if there is a certain amount of cheating on the side!

GEMINI

The dual nature of people born under the Sign of the Twins; Gemini, makes for many complications in love, sex, and marriage. They are interested in at least twice as many pursuits in life as people born under independent (non-double) Signs. These interests include mating, of course. They are the seekers and searchers for stimulation, excitement, change, and variety. Their need for many types of experiences extends to their emotional lives, their mental activities, their hobbies, and their social lives. For this reason, they do not have an easy time in discovering a perfect mate or lover, and without continual stimulation in all these branches of living, boredom soon sets in.

Under the rulership of the planet Mercury, Geminians are more intellectually inclined than passionately so. They prefer activities and pursuits that stimulate the mind to extensions of thought and logic, reasoning removed from the area of the emotions. As well as in other ways, this makes them most eclectic in their choice of a mate or bedmate. They are deep analysts, so that they are not easily pleased. They seem to be forever testing although the candidate for the feelings might never be aware of this. They can be as devious as they are clever.

These sons and daughters of Gemini can be very cold, with over-emotional people, they are distant. With argumentative types, they merely remove themselves from the scene. Those who do not have deep instincts for understanding them will find that just one demonstration of temper will drive the Geminian away permanently.

The elusive personality of the Geminians make them seek a variety of sex partners. They can dissipate their energies in a number of experiences rather than reserving them for the "one and only" that is the dream of members of other Sign groups. They have great personal magnetism and attract members of both sexes who would like to have the thrill of conquering, if only sexually or for a single time, one of these brilliant and charming personalities.

Gemini people do best in marrying or mating with a member of the Virgo group. The tradition is otherwise in astrology, but research by the author shows that the similarity of their natures makes for a good beginning in sharing mental exercise which can evolve into delightful sexual concourse. Eventually all mental and emotional restrictions are dissolved, and a "more perfect union" could hardly be beheld.

The other Air Signs, Libra and Aquarius, are also compatible because they can work out the same or similar destinies. Together they make what is known as a brilliant couple.

A Gemini mating with Pisces is to be avoided because of the demanding nature of the people born under the Sign of the Fish. The Piscean is far too emotional for the cerebral Gemini. The same is true of Gemini-Scorpio combinations. This might be enjoyable and sexually satisfying, even thrilling, but there is not much hope for such a combination to have any permanence. Since Taurus and Capricorn would have little appeal to Gemini, there is little likelihood of mating or marriage except under special conditions and aspects in the individual horoscopes.

CANCER

The people born under the Sign of Cancer are under the rulership of the Moon, one of the two Luminaries, and thus have rather different or unique characters. The most well known and most outstanding of their traits is their changeability. Shakespeare referred to this by calling the situation "as inconstant as the moon." They have intense sensitiveness, are more emotional than intellectual, and they crave love and affection rather than physical sexuality. Love's madness rarely afflicts them, for their ideal is really the comfort of a settled home life. Envy does not afflict them because they cling in spite of everything. They blind themselves to unfaithfulness in their tenacious holding on to what they consider their establishment.

The other Water Signs, Scorpio and Pisces, could rarely if ever join in a happy mating with Cancer. The latter two Signs are people with greater passions, jealousy, hatred, depth of perception that sees even what is not there. Still one should not consider the Moon children to be placid or even-tempered. They are moody, and they respond most profoundly to the phases of their Ruler, the Moon. The viscissitudes of their lives can cause alternating ecstasy and manic depression. These people bear a heavy burden, for in their easy going way they can become the victims of scheming types who plot intrigues and selfish deeds. They have a craving for adventure of which they might be unaware, and their karmic lesson is to try to establish some balance in their emotional and sexual lives.

Cancer folks really discover their sexual potential after fifty. By that time, they have had experience and acquired knowledge. It is best for them to wait for marriage until after the half-century birthday—always depending on the aspects in the native's chart, we repeat.

The ideal partner is a member of the Capricorn Sign group. The Capricornian sexuality, which is both idealistic in its love aspects and deep in its emotional aspects, combined with the clinging vine (male or female) Cancerian type makes for a vivid and romantic attachment. It may not last, but what a time these two will have! If this combination decides to stick together, they will have heaven on earth. Even if they separate there will always be some kind of connection if only a friendly relationship, but it will be for life.

A Cancer woman might find a Gemini man compatible. He would find it agreeable to have his home taken care of, have a bedmate, and be free to go about his other affairs. A Cancer male would not find a Gemini wife too agreeable, as she is inclined to be a run-around, socially or in her own business. Aries and Sagittarius group members would hardly be stimulated by Cancer people, and this combination would become tiresome for both parties. With Leo people, Cancerians could come to a successful working agreement, for here would be a relationship of those ruled by the Moon and by the Sun.

LEO

People born under the Sign of Leo are ruled by the Sun, have sunny dispositions, and are filled with both sex appeal and love. Love is also an element they require in their own lives. Leo is the astrological ruler of the theatre, and its children desire popularity. There is nothing that delights them more than applause—whether they are on the stage or not. They have great glitter and magnetism, tremendous sex appeal, and longevity in life and sexuality.

Leo also rules kingship, as the Sign of royalty and racing. Thus it is easy to understand why Sun children, if they do not want to be luminaries in the theatre, must always be first as king or queen in the family or winner in life's race for success. It makes them somewhat difficult to live with, but at the same time it makes them wonderful company and exciting mates because of their permanently dazzling natures. They are, when in their good moods, generous, sensitive, affectionate, and sympathetic lovers. In their negative moods, they can be vengeful, spiteful, jealous, and recriminative.

In one area of love, Leos have little understanding. Since they feel a sense of being royal, they can never comprehend that their sex partner, lover, or mate is not always in the same mood they are, i.e., ready for love making. In this area, they are unsympathetic and can vent their anger in a vicious way.

Excitement and volcanic emotions are integral parts of Leo's sexual side, and they need to keep control over their feelings. Danger could accompany lack of control, so they must learn to avoid the intrigue and the complicated games they love to play.

Members of the Sign group Scorpio make the best mates for Leo. There is a sexual compatibility in this combination that satisfies the unique craving they both have for sensuous experiences, and great mutual benefits arise from their mating. There is an excitement these two can share that is unequalled in any other combination. It is brought out clearly in the beasts of the zodiac which are their symbols. Leo's is the lion, Scorpio's is the scorpion. Visualized, one sees in the mind's eye two death-dealing creatures of nature. One can readily imagine these two powerful and lethal forces in the struggle for domination, mastery, and sexual eroticism.

For vitality and enthusiasm, members of the Fire Sign groups (which include Leo) are also compatible as there is mutual respect and understanding in the combination. The Leo person can also succeed with a Cancerian as the latter would be eternally grateful and devoted for the attention of such a glittering conquest. Gemini, Libra and Aquarius partners would be too cold to give real happiness to Leo people. While Pisces people are very sexy, they could not match the vitality of Leos. Taurus, Virgo and Capricorn people would be too earthy and material as mates, and Leos should avoid such combinations.

VIRGO

The symbol of the Sign Virgo is the Virgin, one of the rare non-bestial figures in nature's zodiac. It applies, or course, to both males and females. This symbolism stands for a virginal character make-up, but these people are by no means averse˙to sexual intercourse. The symbolism represents their mental attitudes to physical acts.

In actuality, Virgo people are so alert that boredom, and coping with it, are their main problems. For this reason, they leap about both intellectually and sexually. They are excitable, easily aroused, and experimental. As Mercury is the Ruler of their Sign, the best adjective for Virgos is mercurial, synonym for changeable. They pursue many projects, many members of the opposite sex, or their own if homosexual, and have difficulty in settling down and finding happiness.

The sex life of Virgos is more cyclic than most Signs. They have periods of depression and joy alternately, and are emotionally either up or down. Maturing seems to be a long process, but their brilliant minds finally bring them to at least a compromise in their emotional lives; at most, a very sane and rational satisfaction.

Marriage and home life leaves something to be desired if the mate is not of the same fussy type. They like order in their physical surroundings, and are willing to accept responsibility. They are loud complainers when conditions do not please them.

Virgoans make the best of marriages with members of the Leo Sign group. They make a compatible couple mainly because the Virgoans have such a chivalrous and kindly nature that they understand the Leos' need for constant attention. Also, Leos will be very stimulating sexually to Virgoans, and the latter can use such titillation and excitement as they have cycles in which they experience sexual sluggishness. The combination can play most erotic sexual games as the one, Leo, is the hunter, and the other, Virgo, is the prey.

Virgo is an Earth Sign. The other two Earth Signs, Taurus and Capricorn, also provide compatible sex mates and spouses. The qualities of the members of these Signs are similar but astrologically not quite as strong.

People born under the Water Signs bring a warmth and humanity to Virgoans, thus making for a better and more realistic sex life. Thus, Virgo can benefit from mating with Cancer, Scorpio or Pisces.

The other Fire Signs would be too hot for Virgoans to handle, therefore, mating with Aries or Sagittarius should be avoided, or even better, prevented.

LIBRA

Librans love love. They are less interested in the physical sensations and passions of sex than they are in the romantic idea and ideal of what is called "true love." In the deeply emotional sense that Cancer loves, or Scorpio loves, they are lacking profundity of feeling. This statement does not exclude the tact, cooperation, willingness and amiability of the wonderful but limited Libra family.

They also are missing the down-to-earth materialism of the Capricorn type, so that introversion is a general characteristic. This does not mean that they are going to miss happiness, because they can be very much in love with themselves! Secret habits can easily victimize them until they become addicts of some occult or hidden vice.

To the Libran, love is some kind of symbol or representation. It is a drama they are in and observing at one and the same time. To the Librans love is an idealistic intellectual adventure rather than a deep-seated and moving passion; it is something unto itself which consists more of soft lights and music than hot feelings and irresistible physical craving. The fights between lovers that are so great when they make up could never be tolerated by Librans. They would move from the scene, never vindictive, never jealous, just ice cold and distant.

When the situation is under perfect control, the Librans make the best married mates or permanent lovers of all the Signs. Their kindness, gentleness, and courtesy are beyond compare.

Librans are very eclectic in their tastes in sex partners just as they are in all their pursuits in life. They mature early, evolve slowly in the physical aspects of mating, and really enjoy sex to the utmost the older they grow. A great thing about their growth is that it is not a matter of which they are very conscious nor to which they pay much attention. The sons and daughters of Libra are qualified to give a lot of affection to others, and they are not deeply troubled (as so many people born under other Signs) by cravings of a sexual nature. Sex develops slowly but surely.

Librans find the most suitable and compatible mates in the Air Sign Aquarius *plus* (on a lesser scale) the other Air

Sign: Gemini. With an Aquarian mate, the Librans will have a really exciting time both sexually and socially. They stimulate each other, love excessively and satisfy each other fully. The Libra-Gemini combination gives each partner a sense of collusion in love and sex *plus* a unique sense of liberty, freedom, and independence which is also a great source of satisfaction.

The heat of the Fire Signs can also be used for making a good mating with all Librans. Those born under Aries, Leo and Sagittarius combine well with Librans because that vital sexual heat brings warmth to the Librans and balance to the others mentioned. Librans should avoid the Water Signs: Cancer, Scorpio and Pisces, for fear of being endlessly annoyed by their emotional hangups. Finally, Capricorn should be shunned as the Librans would disappear in their ambitious plans and greed.

SCORPIO

In their sexual life and/or in their search for a marriage partner, males and females born under the Sign of Scorpio continue to grow emotionally all the time. They are born with tremendous sex appeal, and usually have experiences at an early age. At the very least, they are much sought after by admirers when they are very young. They are such unusual types, so unique in physical appeal and bodily attraction that even members of their own families have been known to be a threat.

Scorpios become very sophisticated in sexual matters as an outcome of this magnetism. By their middle years, they are likely to "know it all." But this does not make them cold or domineering because it is their nature to mellow with the years. By the time they are senior citizens, the glamor of sex seems to wear off, and they adopt an attitude that seems to ask, "What's all the fuss about?" They are indeed very loveable people!

The sex potential, enormous vitality and virility of the Scorpio-born lead them to experiment in many sexual areas before the whole experiences jades them. They have a sensitive perception and are great game players, fooling others into thinking they are serious or very concerned about conquest. This is the favorite of the sexual games. Scorpios play.

The best mate for a Scorpio person is one born under the Sign of Virgo. This is a situation, or combination, which is unique because the Scorpios need something so different that it will last. Becoming lovers for these two Signs will be another game for the Scorpion to play. The Virgoans will find them fascinating, and this can become a game that lasts for life because of all the different potentials and the variety it offers. There would be many surprises for the Scorpions, something they love, which arises from the peace and sympathy that the Virgoans seem to wear as an aura—one which can finally or eventually enshroud the Scorpion.

The other Water Signs, Cancer and Pisces, also make compatible mates for Scorpions. They share so many traits: unselfishness, emotional profundity, and a sympathy for the occult which makes them so aware of each other's wishes, desires, and secrets. The other Earth Sign group members are also splendid mates for the Scorpions because they (Taurus and Capricorn, besides Virgo) balance the sensitivity of the Scorpios with their earthy, practical outlook on life.

The Air Signs, Gemini, Libra and Aquarius would not fit into the lives of the Scorpions very well because the latter are either too forceful, too concerned with sex, or too demanding. In trying to mate with a member of the Fire Sign groups, the Scorpios could never come to peaceful terms with Aries, Leo or Sagittarius because life between them would be nothing less than a field of competition, rather than a field of cooperative giving or pleasant mutual agreement.

SAGITTARIUS

Sagittarians, male and female, have a longer period of sexual incubation than members of other Signs. They suffer emotional disappointments in their early years because they are not aware, nor made aware, of their innate attractions. Great satisfactions and pleasures usually come after the age of thirty. During this awakening cycle, they stall at getting married. These people are in no rush to attain the matrimonial state. They are further hampered by too much reasoning, too much rational analysis of marriage or having a lover, and too little of the essential sentiments and feelings that establish matrimony as a pleasant and normal experience. These (male and female) Hamlets think too much instead of acting.

Having carefully and reasonably (using their reasoning powers) chosen a mate or permanent lover, they use the same powers of reasoning and analysis to find fault. This can easily mess up a situation that would have worked itself out in time—had time been allowed to do its work. For this reason, multiple marriages as a result of divorce are very common in the Sagittarius Sign group.

Independence is a very important factor in the lives of Sagittarians. They like to be both independent and secretive, and resent any questions or interference in their activities. This is another thorn in the side of any marriage or love affair. They intend, no matter what their vows, to continue their own way of life both inside and outside the home.

The delineation given of the Sagittarius character leads to a single conclusion, that the best mate for Sagittarians is a person born under the Sign Pisces. Combining the traits of these two Signs, there evolves a lessening of the self-centered quality of the Sagittarian and a blooming of the selfless or unselfish Piscean. In a mutuality of interests, the Sagittarians can grow away from their exhibitionist tendencies, their secret interests or even vices, their flaunting of their unique natures. At the same time, the Pisceans can evolve, when married to this Sign, a wonderful spirituality and profound understanding of all living things besides the individual life of the mate.

The Fire Signs also provide compatible mates for the Sagittarians for they are also great enthusiasts, have many diversified interests, and are extremely talented in many areas especially those of a cultural nature. These people of Aries and Leo, (Fire Signs like Sagittarius), understand the depth of the natures of The Archer's children, the bow and arrow being the symbol of the Sagittarians.

Air Sign folks are also compatible to the extent that

they have wide horizons intellectually, and are also able to share the Archers' many interests. Cancer and Scorpio, Water Signs like Pisces, lack the Pisces' profound comprehension of the Sagittarians' need for occasional solitude; they are over-emotional in the wrong direction and possessive. Members of the Earth Sign groups are better as business partners for Sagittarius than as mates.

CAPRICORN

One of the names of the Sign Capricorn is, "the Celestial Schoolmaster." Capricornians are innately teachers, and in the field of sex, they are great teachers, loving the young, loving to rear them, and enjoying the company of youth to the very end of their days. Although they suffer greatly from emotional frustrations, they give great joy all their lives to both young and old.

Their appearance and the impression they make are both deceptive, for they seem cold and distant. In actuality, they crave love and a permanent attachment and/or marriage. Capricorn is an Earth Sign, and those born under it are earthy, indeed. They are sexually greedy, sentimental, generous, analytical, practical, foolhardy, and just a little vengeful—all at the same time. This mixture of traits makes it difficult for people to make friends or lovers of them, for others delude themselves about romance while Capricorn is totally realistic in these areas of their emotional lives.

Capricornians will ponder long and deep before they

take that major step up to the altar. They will walk around the topic, talk around the topic, talk about the topic, and discuss it at great length to the very prospect they have in mind. In the end, they will avoid matrimony or settle for some practical reason such as business or social advancement, money or security. In their hearts, they really want to be taken by storm—an emotional storm of such great upheaval that they experience the profound ecstasy they so deeply yearn for.

The Capricorn personalities should marry or mate with members of the Sign of the Moon, Cancer. Love and passion evolve from this combination of the earthly and the ethereal. A mystic quality is fate's gift to their mating, and each will find that the emotional life they lead together grows in intensity as time goes on. While so different from each other, there is a deep and innate mutual understanding that glues them together rather than separates them.

Capricorn can also get along with members of the other Earth Signs, Taurus and Virgo. These potential combinations can succeed because of the traits they share. They are ambitious to gain wordly goods, respect hard work, and enjoy the rewards of business and the status they attain socially.

The Water Signs, besides Cancer, Scorpio and Pisces are also compatible to Capricornians because they bring out the softer and more gentle traits of the hardboiled and earthy Sign of the Goat.

Gemini, Libra and Aquarius do not mix well with Capricorn. These Sign members are too ephemeral, being Air Signs, for the down-to-earth Capricornians.

There could be little communication between Capricornians and members of the Fire Signs. Aries, Leo and Sagittarius could meet only on commercial fields of endeavor. There would be no chance of a success in romance.

AQUARIUS

The members of the Sign group Aquarius might be considered born lucky. They are ruled by the planet Uranus which is the heavenly deliverer of good things, the star which governs improvements and amelioration on every level throughout life. Having Uranus as the ruling planet, the Uranus-born have a love insurance policy which guarantees sexual pleasure, happiness and satisfaction. They suffer no hangups, no frustrations, no repressions, and rarely any tendency to indulge in any but normal sexual intercourse.

When nature endows so much on the people born under the Sign of the Waterbearer, and they have nothing to complain about, happiness still eludes many of them. They seem not to want what destiny has so richly endowed upon them! Dreams seem to mean more to them than reality, especially where romance is concerned. They talk about love a great deal, and are the most marvelous writers of love letters in the poetic way that they express the emotions they think they are experiencing. Getting all this sentiment into action seems to be quite another—and remote—matter.

Idealism is beautiful, but the Aquarians can stretch a good thing too far. In their search (or waiting for) an ideal romantic lover, they may be passed by. They are far more prepared in this Aquarian Age to put more emphasis on its target, universal love, than upon individual love. Nobody gets married that way!

The universality of love of the Aquarians bar them from a successful mating with members of the Water Signs,

Cancer, Scorpio and Pisces. They are too profoundly filled with feelings and emotions, too easily hurt, too jealous to get along with the easy going Aquarians who never give up trying to better the world around them and the people in it.

The Earth Signs, Taurus, Virgo and Capricorn, would add practicality to the combination, but it would be more suitable to a business partnership than to the legal one known as marriage. The high flights of fancy of the Aquarians would upset the material ideals and ambitions of these people as being too impractical to live with or go to bed with.

Members of the Fire Sign groups, Aries, Leo and Sagittarius could make fairly compatible mates or lovers for Aquarians, since they would be qualified to bring some of their heat to the Waterbearer Sign group.

Aquarians should find their greatest happiness in mating with people born under Libra. This combination would express a joint eroticism, a blending of the balancing power of Libra with the prowess in sex of the Aquarian.

PISCES

To the people born under the Sign of Pisces love is a very great, almost a ruling factor, in their lives. They are extremely sensitive. In fact, the world's greatest mediums and others endowed with psychic power are the astrological children of this Sign governed by the mysterious planet Neptune. They need tight relationships, must be close to others, and especially have one particular individual to adore, to share their lives with, and to lean upon in the spiritual sense. Sometimes they also become learners in the material sense, but this is insignificant to them as they are more other-worldly than worldly in the usual sense of the word.

Fully developed or evolved as mature personalities, the Pisceans can be very sexy. But this takes time, for their minds concentrate on cultural and moral issues while growing up. They neglect their physical and sexual development. Religion also plays a strong role in retarding them from sexual expression even in this age of permissiveness. It is an innate trait that ignores the new liberation the Aquarian Age has brought.

The Pisceans are hard to handle by members of every Sign group. This is the cause of their losing their lovers and mates in so many instances; the lover finds a new love, the mate a distracting affair. The Pisceans make trouble for themselves, too, for in their sensitivity they create untenable situations, then make false accusations based upon them—then seek undeserved consolation in the arms or bed of another. Psychology calls this rationalization.

Growth is the secret to a successful love life and marriage as far as Pisceans are concerned. Since their natural development is slow, the best partner for them is the one who helps them to evolve.

Pisces, greatest success in this department of life comes from mating with someone born under the Sign of the Archer, Sagittarius. The latter can be dazzled by the magnetism and charm, the ineffable appeal of the Piscean. The materialism of the Sagittarians is wonder-struck at the spirituality and otherworldliness of the Pisceans. In the game of sex, the Piscean seems to say, "Catch me if you can." And

Sagittarius, the Archer, reaches for the quiver to draw an arrow, fit it into the bow, and aim for the target!

Cancer and Scorpio, also Water Signs, as is Pisces, are Signs compatible with Pisces. They understand each other, share their sensitivities, and give each other strength.

The Earth Sign people, born under Taurus, Virgo and Capricorn can give virility or fertility or power to the dreamy Pisceans. A combination of any Earth Sign with Pisces will be of more benefit to Pisces than vice versa.

Combined with any of the Air Signs, Gemini, Libra or Aquarius, Pisces would find that only a cold wind blows. On the other hand, from the other Fire Signs, Aries and Leo, Pisces would find too much heat melting them. So, Sagittarius it should be.

MELVIN POWERS SELF-IMPROVEMENT LIBRARY

ASTROLOGY
____ASTROLOGY—HOW TO CHART YOUR HOROSCOPE Max Heindel 7.00
____ASTROLOGY AND SEXUAL ANALYSIS Morris C. Goodman 10.00
____ASTROLOGY AND YOU Carroll Righter 5.00
____ASTROLOGY MADE EASY Astarte 7.00
____ASTROLOGY, ROMANCE, YOU AND THE STARS Anthony Norvell 10.00
____MY WORLD OF ASTROLOGY Sydney Omarr 10.00
____THOUGHT DIAL Sydney Omarr 7.00
____WHAT THE STARS REVEAL ABOUT THE MEN IN YOUR LIFE Thelma White 3.00

BRIDGE
____BRIDGE BIDDING MADE EASY Edwin B. Kantar 15.00
____BRIDGE CONVENTIONS Edwin B. Kantar 10.00
____COMPETITIVE BIDDING IN MODERN BRIDGE Edgar Kaplan 7.00
____DEFENSIVE BRIDGE PLAY COMPLETE Edwin B Kantar 20.00
____GAMESMAN BRIDGE—PLAY BETTER WITH KANTAR Edwin B. Kantar 7.00
____HOW TO IMPROVE YOUR BRIDGE Alfred Sheinwold 7.00
____IMPROVING YOUR BIDDING SKILLS Edwin B. Kantar 10.00
____INTRODUCTION TO DECLARER'S PLAY Edwin B. Kantar 7.00
____INTRODUCTION TO DEFENDER'S PLAY Edwin B. Kantar 10.00
____KANTAR FOR THE DEFENSE Edwin B. Kantar 10.00
____KANTAR FOR THE DEFENSE VOLUME 2 Edwin B. Kantar 10.00
____TEST YOUR BRIDGE PLAY Edwin B. Kantar 10.00
____VOLUME 2—TEST YOUR BRIDGE PLAY Edwin B. Kantar 10.00
____WINNING DECLARER PLAY Dorothy Hayden Truscott 10.00

BUSINESS, STUDY & REFERENCE
____BRAINSTORMING Charles Clark 10.00
____CONVERSATION MADE EASY Elliot Russell 5.00
____EXAM SECRET Dennis B. Jackson 7.00
____FIX-IT BOOK Arthur Symons 2.00
____HOW TO DEVELOP A BETTER SPEAKING VOICE M. Hellier 5.00
____HOW TO SAVE 50% ON GAS & CAR EXPENSES Ken Stansbie 5.00
____HOW TO SELF-PUBLISH YOUR BOOK & MAKE IT A BEST SELLER Melvin Powers .. 20.00
____INCREASE YOUR LEARNING POWER Geoffrey A. Dudley 5.00
____PRACTICAL GUIDE TO BETTER CONCENTRATION Melvin Powers 5.00
____PUBLIC SPEAKING MADE EASY Thomas Montalbo 10.00
____7 DAYS TO FASTER READING William S. Schaill 7.00
____SONGWRITER'S RHYMING DICTIONARY Jane Shaw Whitfield 10.00
____SPELLING MADE EASY Lester D. Basch & Dr. Milton Finkelstein 3.00
____STUDENT'S GUIDE TO BETTER GRADES J.A. Rickard 3.00
____TEST YOURSELF—FIND YOUR HIDDEN TALENT Jack Shafer 3.00
____YOUR WILL & WHAT TO DO ABOUT IT Attorney Samuel G. King 7.00

CALLIGRAPHY
____ADVANCED CALLIGRAPHY Katherine Jeffares 7.00
____CALLIGRAPHY—THE ART OF BEAUTIFUL WRITING Katherine Jeffares 7.00
____CALLIGRAPHY FOR FUN & PROFIT Anne Leptich & Jacque Evans 10.00
____CALLIGRAPHY MADE EASY Tina Serafini 7.00

CHESS & CHECKERS
____BEGINNER'S GUIDE TO WINNING CHESS Fred Reinfeld 10.00
____CHESS IN TEN EASY LESSONS Larry Evans 10.00
____CHESS MADE EASY Milton L. Hanauer 5.00
____CHESS PROBLEMS FOR BEGINNERS Edited by Fred Reinfeld 7.00
____CHESS TACTICS FOR BEGINNERS Edited by Fred Reinfeld 7.00

___HOW TO WIN AT CHECKERS Fred Reinfeld 7.00
___1001 BRILLIANT WAYS TO CHECKMATE Fred Reinfeld 10.00
___1001 WINNING CHESS SACRIFICES & COMBINATIONS Fred Reinfeld 10.00

COOKERY & HERBS
___CULPEPER'S HERBAL REMEDIES Dr. Nicholas Culpeper 5.00
___FAST GOURMET COOKBOOK Poppy Cannon 2.50
___HEALING POWER OF HERBS May Bethel 5.00
___HEALING POWER OF NATURAL FOODS May Bethel 7.00
___HERBS FOR HEALTH—HOW TO GROW & USE THEM Louise Evans Doole 7.00
___HOME GARDEN COOKBOOK—DELICIOUS NATURAL FOOD RECIPES Ken Kraft 3.00
___MEATLESS MEAL GUIDE Tomi Ryan & James H. Ryan, M.D. 4.00
___VEGETABLE GARDENING FOR BEGINNERS Hugh Wilberg 2.00
___VEGETABLES FOR TODAY'S GARDENS R. Milton Carleton 2.00
___VEGETARIAN COOKERY Janet Walker 10.00
___VEGETARIAN COOKING MADE EASY & DELECTABLE Veronica Vezza 3.00

GAMBLING & POKER
___HOW TO WIN AT POKER Terence Reese & Anthony T. Watkins 10.00
___SCARNE ON DICE John Scarne 15.00
___WINNING AT CRAPS Dr. Lloyd T. Commins 5.00
___WINNING AT GIN Chester Wander & Cy Rice 3.00
___WINNING AT POKER—AN EXPERT'S GUIDE John Archer 10.00
___WINNING AT 21—AN EXPERT'S GUIDE John Archer 10.00
___WINNING POKER SYSTEMS Norman Zadeh 10.00

HEALTH
___BEE POLLEN Lynda Lyngheim & Jack Scagnetti 5.00
___COPING WITH ALZHEIMER'S Rose Oliver, Ph.D. & Francis Bock, Ph.D. 10.00
___DR. LINDNER'S POINT SYSTEM FOOD PROGRAM Peter G Lindner, M.D. 2.00
___HELP YOURSELF TO BETTER SIGHT Margaret Darst Corbett 7.00
___HOW YOU CAN STOP SMOKING PERMANENTLY Ernest Caldwell 5.00
___MIND OVER PLATTER Peter G Lindner, M.D. 5.00
___NATURE'S WAY TO NUTRITION & VIBRANT HEALTH Robert J. Scrutton 3.00
___NEW CARBOHYDRATE DIET COUNTER Patti Lopez-Pereira 2.00
___REFLEXOLOGY Dr. Maybelle Segal 7.00
___REFLEXOLOGY FOR GOOD HEALTH Anna Kaye & Don C. Matchan 10.00
___30 DAYS TO BEAUTIFUL LEGS Dr. Marc Selner 3.00
___WONDER WITHIN Thomas S. Coyle, M.D. 10.00
___YOU CAN LEARN TO RELAX Dr. Samuel Gutwirth 5.00

HOBBIES
___BEACHCOMBING FOR BEGINNERS Norman Hickin 2.00
___BLACKSTONE'S MODERN CARD TRICKS Harry Blackstone 7.00
___BLACKSTONE'S SECRETS OF MAGIC Harry Blackstone 7.00
___COIN COLLECTING FOR BEGINNERS Burton Hobson & Fred Reinfeld 7.00
___ENTERTAINING WITH ESP Tony 'Doc' Shiels 2.00
___400 FASCINATING MAGIC TRICKS YOU CAN DO Howard Thurston 7.00
___HOW I TURN JUNK INTO FUN AND PROFIT Sari 3.00
___HOW TO WRITE A HIT SONG AND SELL IT Tommy Boyce 10.00
___MAGIC FOR ALL AGES Walter Gibson 7.00
___PLANTING A TREE TreePeople with Andy & Katie Lipkis 13.00
___STAMP COLLECTING FOR BEGINNERS Burton Hobson 3.00

HORSE PLAYERS' WINNING GUIDES
___BETTING HORSES TO WIN Les Conklin 10.00
___ELIMINATE THE LOSERS Bob McKnight 5.00
___HOW TO PICK WINNING HORSES Bob McKnight 5.00
___HOW TO WIN AT THE RACES Sam (The Genius) Lewin 5.00

____HOW YOU CAN BEAT THE RACES Jack Kavanagh 5.00
____MAKING MONEY AT THE RACES David Barr 7.00
____PAYDAY AT THE RACES Les Conklin 7.00
____SMART HANDICAPPING MADE EASY William Bauman 5.00
____SUCCESS AT THE HARNESS RACES Barry Meadow 7.00

HUMOR

____HOW TO FLATTEN YOUR TUSH Coach Marge Reardon 2.00
____JOKE TELLER'S HANDBOOK Bob Orben 7.00
____JOKES FOR ALL OCCASIONS Al Schock 7.00
____2,000 NEW LAUGHS FOR SPEAKERS Bob Orben 7.00
____2,400 JOKES TO BRIGHTEN YOUR SPEECHES Robert Orben 10.00
____2,500 JOKES TO START'EM LAUGHING Bob Orben 10.00

HYPNOTISM

____CHILDBIRTH WITH HYPNOSIS William S. Kroger, M.D. 5.00
____HOW TO SOLVE YOUR SEX PROBLEMS WITH SELF-HYPNOSIS Frank Caprio, M.D. . . . 5.00
____HOW YOU CAN BOWL BETTER USING SELF-HYPNOSIS Jack Heise 7.00
____HOW YOU CAN PLAY BETTER GOLF USING SELF-HYPNOSIS Jack Heise 3.00
____HYPNOSIS AND SELF-HYPNOSIS Bernard Hollander, M.D. 7.00
____HYPNOTISM (Originally published 1893) Carl Sextus 5.00
____HYPNOTISM MADE EASY Dr. Ralph Winn. 7.00
____HYPNOTISM MADE PRACTICAL Louis Orton 5.00
____HYPNOTISM REVEALED Melvin Powers 3.00
____MODERN HYPNOSIS Lesley Kuhn & Salvatore Russo, Ph.D. 5.00
____NEW CONCEPTS OF HYPNOSIS Bernard C. Gindes, M.D. 10.00
____NEW SELF-HYPNOSIS Paul Adams 10.00
____POST-HYPNOTIC INSTRUCTIONS—SUGGESTIONS FOR THERAPY Arnold Furst . . . 10.00
____PRACTICAL GUIDE TO SELF-HYPNOSIS Melvin Powers 10.00
____PRACTICAL HYPNOTISM Philip Magonet, M.D. 3.00
____SECRETS OF HYPNOTISM S.J. Van Pelt, M.D. 5.00
____SELF-HYPNOSIS—A CONDITIONED-RESPONSE TECHNIQUE Laurence Sparks 7.00
____SELF-HYPNOSIS—ITS THEORY, TECHNIQUE & APPLICATION Melvin Powers 7.00
____THERAPY THROUGH HYPNOSIS Edited by Raphael H. Rhodes 5.00

JUDAICA

____SERVICE OF THE HEART Evelyn Garfiel, Ph.D. 10.00
____STORY OF ISRAEL IN COINS Jean & Maurice Gould 2.00
____STORY OF ISRAEL IN STAMPS Maxim & Gabriel Shamir 1.00
____TONGUE OF THE PROPHETS Robert St. John 10.00

JUST FOR WOMEN

____COSMOPOLITAN'S GUIDE TO MARVELOUS MEN Foreword by Helen Gurley Brown . . 3.00
____COSMOPOLITAN'S HANG-UP HANDBOOK Foreword by Helen Gurley Brown 4.00
____COSMOPOLITAN'S LOVE BOOK—A GUIDE TO ECSTASY IN BED 7.00
____COSMOPOLITAN'S NEW ETIQUETTE GUIDE Foreword by Helen Gurley Brown 4.00
____I AM A COMPLEAT WOMAN Doris Hagopian & Karen O'Connor Sweeney 3.00
____JUST FOR WOMEN—A GUIDE TO THE FEMALE BODY Richard E. Sand M.D. 5.00
____NEW APPROACHES TO SEX IN MARRIAGE John E. Eichenlaub, M.D. 3.00
____SEXUALLY ADEQUATE FEMALE Frank S. Caprio, M.D. 3.00
____SEXUALLY FULFILLED WOMAN Dr. Rachel Copelan 5.00

MARRIAGE, SEX & PARENTHOOD

____ABILITY TO LOVE Dr. Allan Fromme 7.00
____GUIDE TO SUCCESSFUL MARRIAGE Drs. Albert Ellis & Robert Harper 10.00
____HOW TO RAISE AN EMOTIONALLY HEALTHY, HAPPY CHILD Albert Ellis, Ph.D. 10.00
____PARENT SURVIVAL TRAINING Marvin Silverman, Ed.D. & David Lustig, Ph.D. 10.00
____POTENCY MIRACLE Uri P. Peles, M.D. 10.00
____SEX WITHOUT GUILT Albert Ellis, Ph.D. 7.00

_____ SEXUALLY ADEQUATE MALE Frank S. Caprio, M.D. 3.00
_____ SEXUALLY FULFILLED MAN Dr. Rachel Copelan 5.00
_____ STAYING IN LOVE Dr. Norton F. Kristy 7.00

MELVIN POWERS MAIL ORDER LIBRARY
_____ HOW TO GET RICH IN MAIL ORDER Melvin Powers 20.00
_____ HOW TO SELF-PUBLISH YOUR BOOK Melvin Powers 20.00
_____ HOW TO WRITE A GOOD ADVERTISEMENT Victor O. Schwab 20.00
_____ MAIL ORDER MADE EASY J. Frank Brumbaugh 20.00
_____ MAKING MONEY WITH CLASSIFIED ADS Melvin Powers 20.00

METAPHYSICS & OCCULT
_____ CONCENTRATION—A GUIDE TO MENTAL MASTERY Mouni Sadhu 10.00
_____ EXTRA-TERRESTRIAL INTELLIGENCE—THE FIRST ENCOUNTER 6.00
_____ FORTUNE TELLING WITH CARDS P. Foli 10.00
_____ HOW TO INTERPRET DREAMS, OMENS & FORTUNE TELLING SIGNS Gettings 5.00
_____ HOW TO UNDERSTAND YOUR DREAMS Geoffrey A. Dudley 7.00
_____ MAGICIAN—HIS TRAINING AND WORK W.E. Butler 7.00
_____ MEDITATION Mouni Sadhu 10.00
_____ MODERN NUMEROLOGY Morris C. Goodman 5.00
_____ NUMEROLOGY—ITS FACTS AND SECRETS Ariel Yvon Taylor 5.00
_____ NUMEROLOGY MADE EASY W. Mykian 5.00
_____ PALMISTRY MADE EASY Fred Gettings 7.00
_____ PALMISTRY MADE PRACTICAL Elizabeth Daniels Squire 7.00
_____ PROPHECY IN OUR TIME Martin Ebon 2.50
_____ SUPERSTITION—ARE YOU SUPERSTITIOUS? Eric Maple 2.00
_____ TAROT OF THE BOHEMIANS Papus 10.00
_____ WAYS TO SELF-REALIZATION Mouni Sadhu 7.00
_____ WITCHCRAFT, MAGIC & OCCULTISM—A FASCINATING HISTORY W.B. Crow 10.00
_____ WITCHCRAFT—THE SIXTH SENSE Justine Glass 7.00

RECOVERY
_____ KNIGHT IN RUSTY ARMOR Robert Fisher 5.00
_____ KNIGHT IN RUSTY ARMOR (Hard cover edition) Robert Fisher 10.00
_____ KNIGHTS WITHOUT ARMOR (Hard cover edition) Aaron R. Kipnis, Ph.D. 10.00
_____ PRINCESS WHO BELIEVED IN FAIRY TALES Marcia Grad 10.00

SELF-HELP & INSPIRATIONAL
_____ CHANGE YOUR VOICE, CHANGE YOUR LIFE Morton Cooper, Ph.D. 10.00
_____ CHARISMA—HOW TO GET "THAT SPECIAL MAGIC" Marcia Grad 10.00
_____ DAILY POWER FOR JOYFUL LIVING Dr. Donald Curtis 7.00
_____ DYNAMIC THINKING Melvin Powers 5.00
_____ GREATEST POWER IN THE UNIVERSE U.S. Andersen 10.00
_____ GROW RICH WHILE YOU SLEEP Ben Sweetland 10.00
_____ GROW RICH WITH YOUR MILLION DOLLAR MIND Brian Adams 7.00
_____ GROWTH THROUGH REASON Albert Ellis, Ph.D. 10.00
_____ GUIDE TO PERSONAL HAPPINESS Albert Ellis, Ph.D. & Irving Becker, Ed.D. 10.00
_____ HANDWRITING ANALYSIS MADE EASY John Marley 10.00
_____ HANDWRITING TELLS Nadya Olyanova 7.00
_____ HOW TO ATTRACT GOOD LUCK A.H.Z. Carr 10.00
_____ HOW TO DEVELOP A WINNING PERSONALITY Martin Panzer 10.00
_____ HOW TO DEVELOP AN EXCEPTIONAL MEMORY Young & Gibson 10.00
_____ HOW TO LIVE WITH A NEUROTIC Albert Ellis, Ph.D. 10.00
_____ HOW TO MAKE A $100,000 A YEAR IN SALES Albert Winnikoff 15.00
_____ HOW TO OVERCOME YOUR FEARS M.P. Leahy, M.D. 3.00
_____ HOW TO SUCCEED Brian Adams 10.00
_____ HUMAN PROBLEMS & HOW TO SOLVE THEM Dr. Donald Curtis 5.00
_____ I CAN Ben Sweetland 10.00
_____ I WILL Ben Sweetland 10.00